Lifelong Learning in Museums
A European Handbook

Edited by Kirsten Gibbs, Margherita Sani, Jane Thompson

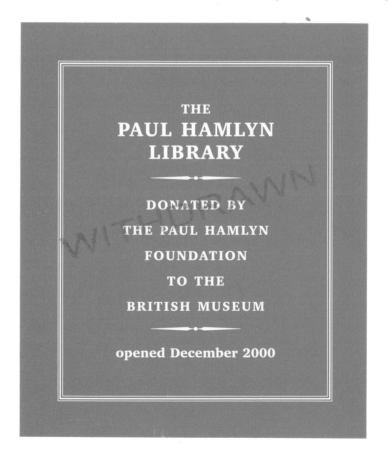

CONTRIBUTORS

David Anderson, Judi Caton, Cristina Da Milano, Martina De Luca, Juliette Fritsch,
Kirsten Gibbs, Rinske Jurgens, Kaija Kaitavuori, Hanneke Kempen,
Andrea Kieskamp, Massimo Negri, Margaret O'Brien, Helen O'Donoghue,
Carla Padró, Margarida Ruas, Margherita Sani, Dineke Stam, Jane Thompson,
Ineke van Klink, Annemarie Vels Heijn, Amber Walls, Sue Wilkinson

ACKNOWLEDGMENTS

Valeria Cicala
Margriet de Jong
Valentina Galloni
Alex Hitchins
Els Hoogstraat
Judikje Kiers
Silvia Mascheroni
Shriti Patel
Anna Pironti
Carlo Tovoli

DESIGN

Oliver Newbery

(over page) From the catalogue of the exhibition Gli occhi del pubblico
(Bologna, IBC-CLUEB, 2006)

Photo: Tano d'Amico

Contents

Foreword

Anyone who has worked on a trans-national museum project which aims to create something practical and useful, knows how difficult this can be. Differences of language, culture and intellectual traditions become more evident, the deeper one goes into the project. The dominance of a limited number of European languages – and, in particular, English – often creates an unequal basis for communication. Even the definition of a "museum" differs from country to country.

This handbook is a persuasive statement of the great value of internationalism despite such difficulties. If we are to develop our professional practice, we need a greater diversity of models than our own country alone can supply. By working together, face to face over an extended period of time, we can go beyond superficial perceptions and develop a more profound understanding of the value of both commonality and difference.

Through research and publication, perceptions can be challenged and developed. So this handbook is also a statement of the importance of critical enquiry in learning from professional practice in other countries.

It is tempting to think that the many examples of innovative work in this publication are the norm in European museums, the standard that should be expected of all public institutions in a democracy. If it were the case, this book would not be necessary. But "Lifelong Learning in Museums" is also a statement of hope. Good practice is widespread, and it is growing.

David Anderson
Director of Learning and Interpretation
Victoria and Albert Museum
London

Self test

Photo: Het Dolhuys Museum, Haarlem

Introduction

Lifelong Museum Learning

This handbook grows out of Lifelong Museum Learning (LLML), a two year project funded by the European Commission between October 2004 and December 2006 within the framework of the Socrates Grundtvig programme. European projects are collective enterprises which, while aiming at common goals, take into account and mediate between different viewpoints and perspectives arising from the history, background and working practices of the individuals and the countries involved, as well as the learning process which takes place during the project. As a consequence, the outcomes of such projects reflect these diversities, and at the same time try to harmonise them into one coherent whole. This handbook is conceived in a way that, while drawing from the richness and variety of experiences that Europe can offer, tries to speak to the reader with one voice.

It must be said, however, that, although all contributors work internationally, the handbook draws mainly on the experiences of partners within their own country, where they have more detailed knowledge.

Lifelong Museum Learning developed and ran training addressed to museum educators and cultural mediators working with adults. During its lifespan four training courses were organised by partner institutions in the project: two test ones, held in Italy in October 2005 and two more, open to wider participation through the Comenius Grundtvig catalogue, in Portugal (May 2006) and in the Netherlands (November 2006). The subject addressed by LLML aroused great interest among museum professionals throughout Europe, especially at a time when the museum's role is widening and stretching to embrace and support lifelong learning, social change, intercultural dialogue, often involving new audiences.

Our intention was that the project should not only benefit those who were able to take part in the training events, but that it should reach as many people as possible, hence the idea of a handbook as part of the project's dissemination strategy.

Language and terminology

When working in a European context, one of the first difficulties to be encountered has to do with the language, as the same words have different connotations in different contexts. As some expressions recur frequently in this handbook, which might mean different things to different readers, it might be useful to state here the meaning we attach to them.

- **Lifelong learning:** learning in which we engage throughout our lives
- **Formal learning:** learning that takes place in a formal education or training setting, normally leading to a qualification
- **Non-formal learning:** learning that is structured and organised but does not lead to a qualification
- **Informal learning:** learning that occurs through family, social or civic life, not necessarily intentionally

As for the meaning of the word **learning**, our group adopted the definition used by the UK Campaign for Learning, which reads: "Learning is a process of active engagement with experience. It is what people do when they want to make sense of the world. It may involve an increase in skills, knowledge, understanding, values, feelings, attitudes and capacity to reflect. Effective learning leads to change, development and the desire to learn more."

Finally, when we use the expression **museums**, we mean all types of museums, including art galleries.

Who is this handbook for?

This handbook is designed to support museum and gallery staff, especially those who have responsibility for education, interpretation or access, ensuring that learning opportunities, exhibitions, and resources are genuinely open to all. It is also for those educators who are more familiar with methodologies and practice relating to schoolchildren and would like to expand education activities to include adults. The publication is aimed at a broad European audience, with a variety of specialist training, expertise, experience, and status within their organisations. Some

sections will be more relevant than others, depending on individual situations and needs. In the same way, some suggestions for good practice will be easier to implement than others.

This publication assumes that readers would like to see equal opportunities placed at the heart of museum provision, to open up access and to invite wider participation, and offers some suggestions and examples for how to achieve this. These include a more pro-active approach to visitor research and outreach initiatives, a commitment to understanding how adults learn and what they wish to achieve from learning within the museum environment, and a willingness to identify and remove institutional barriers that may hinder non-traditional visitors from making use of the learning opportunities and resources a museum can offer.

We hope this handbook will be used as a tool to help programme planning and delivery as well as longer-term strategic planning. We also envisage its use within training contexts, as we acknowledge the value of targeted, relevant training and also of sharing practice with colleagues, both in

one's own country and internationally, through continuing professional development and informal networking.

We welcome readers' views on this handbook, as well as on future sector training needs. Contacts can be made to the leading partner or to any of the project's partners.

Kirsten Gibbs
Margherita Sani
Jane Thompson

(over page) From the catalogue of the exhibition Gli occhi del pubblico (Bologna, IBC-CLUEB, 2006)

Photo: Tano d'Amico

Section 1

'A would-be civilised democracy will not abuse culture for immediate political ends, nor impose its own pre-determined definition of culture on its people. It will be open, democratic, not bullying nor endlessly all-things-to-all-men-or-women. It will offer perspectives on the better and the best; its citizens will be free to be both inside and outside their own cultural overcoats.'

Richard Hoggart

Photo: Leicester Arts and Museum Service

1.1 Lifelong learning

Lifelong Learning is a familiar term throughout Europe but, as with other concepts that exist in a range of different cultural traditions and contexts, it can mean different things to different people. This handbook defines lifelong learning in two ways.

The first is to highlight the importance and significance of learning throughout life, as distinct from the kind of education directed at school-age and college students. In this handbook we are focusing on the learning that adult visitors (i.e. those over 16 years of age) can experience in museums.

The second usage has to do with what is meant by learning. Formal   implies an exchange between teachers and students, in which the students are instructed by the teachers. Lifelong learning puts the emphasis on the activity of the recipients. It may occur in response to formal instruction but it also takes place in a variety of other ways and settings, including everyday lives, interactions with other people and cultural opportunities.

What characterises lifelong learning is that it happens everywhere, not simply in schools, colleges, or universities. When it happens in public and cultural spaces like museums or art galleries – it happens through choice rather than compulsion. It often happens informally, without the need for accreditation, qualification, or measurement. Museums can be ideal places for promoting informal learning. Visitors may leave a museum knowing more than when they arrived: knowledge, understanding, insight or inspiration that helps to make a positive difference to their lives.

1.2 Adult learners

Lifelong learning within a museum can be informal, casual, or even accidental as far as the learner is concerned, however educators and other museum staff must still adopt a formal and rigorous approach to devising learning opportunities, taking into consideration some of the characteristics of adult learners.

Methodologies working with school groups are well-established and museums have a wealth of experience in this area – from making contact with teachers, devising programmes to support and enhance the formal curriculum, and employing a variety of learning styles. Much of this good practice translates to adult learners in the museum. For example, both adults and children:

- Would like to be treated with courtesy and respect

- Enjoy contributing their own knowledge, experience and opinions to the learning process

- Appreciate having an element of choice in the learning process

- Do not want to be talked down to or patronised.

There is one great difference between children and adult learners: children and young people go to school and college because they have to. Adults are more likely to get involved in learning because they want to know about something that interests them, or because they need to learn about something for their jobs or in relation to their families and communities. Learning is for a purpose. It is less about memorising facts and pre-digested information and more about exploring new ideas and experiences, weighing up the evidence and coming to some tentative conclusions. It involves developing practical skills and discovering hidden talents. Some of the main characteristics that make adults different from children when it comes to learning are as follows. All of these are relevant to learning in museums.

- Adult learners are autonomous and self-directed. They need to be able to direct themselves and be actively involved in the learning process. They have to choose what they want to learn and to work on projects and subject-matter that reflect their interests.

- Adults have accumulated life experiences and knowledge including work-related activities, family responsibilities, life-changing challenges, personal passions and previous education. New learning is most effective and successful when it starts from, and is connected to, adults' existing knowledge and experience. The starting place for new learning should build upon existing strengths and experience but not, of course, be restricted to what they already know.

- Adults are goal-oriented. When they start a formal learning activity, they usually know what they want to achieve and where they want to get to. In formal learning situations adults generally appreciate an education programme that is well organised and has clearly defined elements. In informal learning situations, adults learn best when the signposts are clear, the purpose is relevant and interesting and when their emotions (such as curiosity, anger, wonder, pleasure) are engaged.

- Adults are relevancy-oriented. For most adults, learning has to be relevant to their interests, their lives, their work or other responsibilities. Again, learning should start where people are. Once they are stimulated and eager to learn more, then there is every chance that what they regard as interesting and relevant will be greatly expanded.

- Adult learners often start out by being practical, and want to focus on those things that are most useful to them in their work or lives. At first they may not be interested in knowledge for its own sake but once they get the learning bug they often want to learn about all kinds of things that were previously outside their experience.

- Like all learners, adults need to be shown respect: they should be treated as equals in experience and knowledge and encouraged to voice their opinions freely in every learning situation.

1.3 Barriers to learning

The reasons most frequently given by potential learners for not getting involved in learning –and this applies also to museum and gallery settings - are practical ones that arise from their individual and immediate circumstances: financial costs, time constraints related to employment or family, ill-health or disability, transport or childcare difficulties, lack of local opportunities.

Research evidence shows that the major obstacles can also be cultural, social or psychological. These include a dislike of school as a child, or a social class or gender belief which does not see learning as an appropriate activity for adults in a particular group. These are harder barriers to overcome because they involve feelings and assumptions and are based on deeply held values and attitudes.

1.4 Attitudes and motivations that lead to learning

What makes the difference? Why do some adults decide to get involved in learning? Knowing the answer to this question can help museum educators think about how they approach adult visitors. Research into adult learning generally agrees about what motivates adults to be interested in learning. Attitudes are strongly influenced by family and cultural background, social class, gender, school experiences and social networks. Though not all of the reasons apply strictly to learning in museums, they are useful to keep in mind when designing learning programmes and situations for adults in museum and galleries.

- Family: to help children and to understand better what their children are learning at school. Joining family learning programmes often motivates parents to learn for their own benefit.

- Social: to make new friends, to meet the need for social association and friendship.

- Educational progression: to get a qualification or to move on to a more demanding course.

- To settle and contribute to communities – to take a more active role in their communities. This is especially true for newly arrived immigrants, refugees, asylum seekers, and migrant workers.

- The example and encouragement of other people: family, friends, workmates or education professionals, community or guidance workers, and employers.

- Involvement in community action or in voluntary and community groups and organizations: involving the development and practice of skills and the celebration of identity and culture.

- Work: to get a better job and to improve performance at work.

- Personal development reasons – to improve their knowledge and skills, to pursue an interest or hobby.

- A life change or crisis: migration, bereavement, illness, redundancy, house move, divorce, retirement.

- Compulsion or requirement: by an employer or the state, such as changes in work practices, welfare benefit regulations and naturalisation requirements.

1.5 Equality and access

Museums in Europe are popular places, visited each year by millions of people. Visitors come because they are interested in history, art or culture, searching for significance and identity, looking for inspiration, or to learn something about the objects on display. Some come because museums are the places to visit when you are exploring a new city or have some free time. They are places of pleasure, leisure, entertainment and learning.

But for the many people who visit museums, there are others – a majority of the population – who rarely or never do so. In general, museum visitors are likely to have higher social, economic and educational status than non-visitors. Those who are poor, those who have been less well served by formal education, those who are members of minority groups that are already disadvantaged or discriminated against in society do not easily recognise museums as public places which they are entitled to visit. They may believe that museums are for other people and not for them. Too often museums are not as welcoming and accessible to their non-traditional visitors as they might be.

At European level, it can also be said that museums, when developing educational programmes or activities, generally focus on school groups, rather than the adult population. Given the acknowledged educational role of museums, and the understanding of governments at both national and European level of the importance of lifelong learning, this needs to be addressed.

The expectation that museums should play a part in public education, in widening participation and access, and in somehow ameliorating the human condition through the pleasure or insight to be derived from what they have to offer, remains contentious in some quarters.

Choosing to make education and equality a high priority in museums means:

- Developing an accessible and learning friendly environment, which encourages visitors and supports learning.

- Taking a multi-layered approach to display and interpretation, so that everyone from the first-time visitor to the academic feels welcome.

- Ensuring that museum staff are as informed and rigorous in their knowledge about visitors, as they are about collections and exhibitions.

- Considering display so that exhibits provide access, in all senses, to diverse audiences.

- Making the existing educational levels and learning styles of potential visitors the starting point for targeted education work within the museum.

- Reviewing and modifying some of the conventions of museums in order to be welcoming to new visitors.

- Ensuring that the diversity of staff reflects the diversity of the audience the museum wishes to attract.

Section 2

Learning in Museums

'Everyone has the right freely to participate in the cultural life of the community, to enjoy the arts and to share in scientific advancement and its benefits'

Article 27, Universal Declaration of Human Rights

Participants in adult programme Charcoal and Chocolate 2004

Photo: Irish Museum of Modern Art, Dublin

2.1 Setting the scene

The gap between museums and their potential audiences was probably smaller in the 19th century. At that time, museums across Europe had a specific role in society which included the representation of power, the creation of national identity, and the educational and moral improvement of the masses. But in Britain, for example, although cultural organisations set their sights on the respectable poor, they drew the line at criminals, vagrants and those residents in the poor house. Library rules enforcing clean hands and faces were often rigorously applied to counteract fears about the transmission of disease and contagion through books. And although they were originally intended to improve and educate the masses, museums soon assumed more middle class connotations which continue to influence contemporary cultures and audiences. By the end of the nineteenth century the educators and improvers had been effectively marginalised and aesthetes and academics were in the ascendancy.

This shift in focus largely remains, although in some countries, for example the UK and the Netherlands, the demand for arts and cultural learning in museums has assumed greater prominence on the cultural and political agenda, especially in relation to non-traditional audiences. In other European countries, museums open up to new audiences on their own initiative or as a response to community requests, despite the absence of a political agenda promoting this.

Whether for political, cultural or institutional reasons, museums take on many roles: including being agents of social change, with responsibilities for social inclusion and community development, as well as supporting scientific development and lifelong learning.

The quality and provision of education programmes for adults in European museums varies enormously. In some institutions programmes are well-developed and often include accredited courses, practical workshops, guided visits, discussions, lectures or family events. In others, education is still seen as an 'add-on', with token attempts to attract non-traditional learners pursued as one-off projects, operating on the margins of the museums' main concerns.

Learning in museums is different from the learning which takes place in formal education establishments since most learners are informal ones. On the whole, museums are unaware of the learning objectives of their users: whether it is for pleasure, in relation to a special interest, or in pursuit of identity and cultural meaning. Visitors may not view their visit to a museum as a learning experience, as such, even though they may be learning whilst enjoying themselves. Regular visitors are attracted by the informality of the visit and the fact that taking part does not require too great a commitment of time or money. For those who find museums alien places, however, the atmosphere can seem immensely formal and daunting, and the commitment needed to make such a visit may well be both costly and considerable.

The outcomes of museum learning experiences are equally diverse. Among the most positive outcomes are increased knowledge and understanding, the development of new skills and abilities, and the inspiration to learn more. Quite often learners use their visits to museums to reinforce the knowledge they already have and to share this with other people, for example, with their children. Learners who find a connection at the museum with their interests, experience or sense of themselves in the world are more likely to re-visit than learners who do not make that connection.

2.2 Approaches to learning in museums

The provision of learning opportunities in museums should be based on the application of learning theories and successful methodologies and practice with adult learners. It is also quite often predicated on strongly held cultural, institutional or personal assumptions by museum staff towards visitors. Broadly speaking there are four main approaches to learning in museums, any combination of which may be in use at the same time:

- **Instructive or didactic**
- **Active or discovery learning**
- **Constructivist**
- **Social constructionist**

THE INSTRUCTIVE OR DIDACTIC APPROACH

In this approach the museum regards itself as the teacher and visitors as a largely passive and receptive audience. The institutional culture tends to be hierarchical with great respect given to expert knowledge, at the expense of informal or everyday knowledge. Mediators or guides may act as the messengers of specialists in the transmission of pre-decided information to learners. This approach underpins, for example, the traditional guided tour.

The advantage of the didactic approach is that it focuses on delivery of content which can be quickly assimilated or memorised – the 'facts' about a work of art or an object. The disadvantage of this approach is that knowledge is selected by 'experts' and assumes that visitors will learn what has been selected, with little room for discussion: learning is seen as fixed and cumulative, and knowledge regarded as neutral, objective and universal. The didactic approach does not allow for different learning styles, since content is transmitted as though everyone learns in the same way. Some museums have modified

Participants in workshop for older people in association with the National Theatre

Photo: Irish Museum of Modern Art, Dublin

their guided visits to ask questions of the audience, both to determine prior levels of knowledge and to involve the audience more actively in the learning process.

THE ACTIVE OR DISCOVERY LEARNING APPROACH

Active learning became popular in the science museums of the 1970s, and has since become common in other types of museum. Adopting a discovery learning standpoint suggests that the museum believes that learning will happen best in a relaxed, informal atmosphere, where the distinctions between education and entertainment are blurred or merged. Museum staff are frequently organised into teams of complementary professionals who develop both exhibits and education content. Learning is regarded as a process of inquiry that involves role-playing and activity-based, direct participation by learners, who are seen as participants rather than a passive audience. Great use is made of hands-on and interactive learning experiences. It is this approach to learning that underpins interactive exhibits in many contemporary museums.

THE CONSTRUCTIVIST APPROACH

When museums adopt a constructivist approach, the institution becomes a forum in which there can be many different kinds of learning experiences for different visitors. The focus is on the learner rather than the exhibit or the subject content. Museum staff work in teams and visitor knowledge is integrated through evaluation and the activity of audience advocates. Learning is regarded as an active process, as well as a social activity within a specific context. Since learners bring their own perspectives, values and experiences, museum educators seek to provide different kinds of learning opportunities through different exhibition styles, learning styles and levels of engagement. It is this approach to learning that underpins the application of Kolb's theories to learning in some Dutch museums, described below.

THE SOCIAL CONSTRUCTIONIST APPROACH

This approach assumes that museums are sites in which social, cultural, historical and political knowledge is constructed and negotiated. Visitors are seen as interpreters who have the right to negotiate this knowledge according to their own identity and position in society. In this context the learners' class, gender, race, ethnicity, sexuality, religion, and so on become of vital importance to what they bring to bear on their interpretation of knowledge. The context is assumed to be more important than the exhibit or the content. Knowledge is regarded as fluid – in the post-modern sense – in that it is created out of struggle and conflict and is subject to constant change and re-negotiation. It is this approach to learning that has influenced attempts to include learners' voices and personal narratives directly in the creation of multi-cultural exhibitions.

2.3 Learning theories: understanding how adults learn

Given these different approaches to museum education, some understanding of how adults learn is an important starting point for museum educators. A familiarity with and application of learning theories within exhibitions, programmes and activities enables a museum to become more responsive than was traditionally the case, with a greater appeal to people with different backgrounds, learning styles and intelligences.

Adults tend to learn in different ways, bringing different amounts of knowledge or experiences with them to the learning situation, therefore museums that want to stimulate learning need to focus on learners and find ways of putting them at the heart of what is to be experienced. During the last ten years or so, much work has been done in museums and higher education institutions developing successful methodologies, learning from good practice, and sharing success with colleagues. The best museums have paid increased attention to visitor research and preferences, developing successful ways of working with their audiences by the application of learning theories and learning styles.

LEARNING THEORIES APPLIED TO MUSEUMS

Most learning theories are products of the 1970s and 1980s, when interests in social psychology and learning led to a multitude of learning theories.

See for a survey www. funderstanding.com/theories.cfm

Most of these theories – associated with Jean Piaget, Jerome Bruner, Benjamin Bloom David Ausubel and Howard Gardener, for example - have been developed further over the years and are still used to a greater or lesser extent in formal and informal education, coaching and training. Though most of them deal with learning at schools and universities and in adult education, some have found their way into museum education, especially in connection with the instruction of children and young people.

One of the theories that became popular in museums in the 1970s was **Jean Piaget**'s theory of the four stages of development:

- Sensimotor stage of learning – birth to 2 years old

- Pre-operational stage: language and symbolic representations – 2 to 7 years

- Concrete operations: abstract reasoning, based on personal experiences – 7 to 11 years

- Formal operations: hypotheses and analysis of abstract notions – 11 to 15 years and above.

Piaget's ideas were further elaborated by **Jerome Bruner** who also described the three different ways of learning which adults use alternatively to learn something new:

- The performing mode: to do things

- The expressive mode: to make a mental image; to make connections

- The symbolic mode: where learning is separated from the concrete (Whether a person uses this last mode depends on age and intellectual capacities).

Another learning theory that became prominent in education and was also used in museum education in the 1970s and 1980s (and is still in use in some areas) was **Benjamin Bloom**'s theory of the three learning domains:

- Cognitive learning: the acquisition and organisation of knowledge

- Affective learning: the instinctive incorporation of knowledge and attitudes

- Psychomotor stage learning: the acquisition of skills.

Some educators at the time became interested in theory that people (children) learn better if beforehand 'advanced organisers' are offered. This became the basis of the methodology which combines an introduction to the subject in the classroom, followed by more information and experiential learning in the museum.

At the moment one of the most popular learning theories is that of **Howard Gardner**, the first version of which was first presented in the 1980s, but which is still being developed and expanded.

Gardner's theory is based on the conviction that learning and teaching should focus on the particular intelligences of each person. He discerns eight intelligences:

- **Verbal Linguistic**
- **Logical Mathematical**
- **Musical**
- **Spatial**
- **Bodily Kinesthetic**
- **Interpersonal**
- **Intrapersonal**
- **Naturalistic**

Everyone possesses all of these intelligences but some qualities are more prominent than others. What intelligences a person develops depends on genetics and also on cultural background. Some museums employ Gardner's multiple intelligences theory, both in education programmes and in the display and interpretation of objects.

A theory especially prominent in professional development and management, is the **Myer Briggs Type Indicator (MBTI).** It is, strictly speaking, a personality theory, but since learning has a lot to do with people's personality, it is relevant to museum education. In the MBTI, Isabel Myers defined personality types, based on four dimensions:

- **Extroversion versus introversion**
- **Sensing versus intuition**
- **Thinking versus feeling**
- **Judging versus perceptive**

The resulting combinations can indicate 16 personality types.

See:
www.personalitypathways.com

Paulo Freire, on the other hand, is more concerned with the kinds of knowledge that can assist people to change their lives and change their world through liberatory learning. He is probably the most influential and radical thinker about informal and popular education in the twentieth century. His work in Brazil, until he died in 1997, gained him an international reputation that has inspired and informed countless others across the world to make use of his ideas and methods. Freire made observations about 'banking' education, in which learners are passive and have ready-made knowledge 'deposited' in their minds, thereby maintaining a culture of silence, in which dominated individuals lose the means to respond to the culture forced on them by more dominant members of their society.

From the catalogue of the exhibition Gli occhi del pubblico (Bologna, IBC-CLUEB, 2006)

Photo: Isabella Balena

Freire's dialogical method is based on a cooperative, two-way approach to learning, which emphasises the interchangeability of teachers and learners. Once learners become increasingly aware of the roots of their oppression within the culture of silence, they develop the kind of critical consciousness that enables them to become empowered and to take part in collective action, leading to personal and social change. In the process the world becomes less oppressive and more fully humanised, which is the historical task of any movement concerned with liberation.

KOLB'S LEARNING THEORY AND ITS APPLICATION TO MUSEUMS

In this book we are exploring Kolb's theory in greater depth than the others, because it has recently been applied in several museums, especially in the Netherlands. It is therefore possible to see the implications and consequences of its employment in the planning and staging of exhibitions, interpretation materials and education programmes.

David Kolb's theory of different learning styles is outlined in his book *Experiential Learning*. The impact of his ideas has been significant in the context of liberal adult education, but remains less well known in museum education. His relatively simple proposition is that not everyone learns in the same way. He suggests that everyone has a preferred learning style, or sometimes a combination of more than one learning style, out of a possible total of four. An individual's preferred learning style determines how he or she goes about the learning process. Kolb's ideas seem to relate well to what happens in museums, in that visitors demonstrate different ways of approaching exhibitions because they have different preferred learning styles. Very often they do not approach the exhibition in the way in which it was conceived or designed. Therefore, in order to create the best possible opportunity for learning to take place, it would seem important that the staging of exhibitions and presentations in museums should offer ingredients that connect to each kind of learning style.

According to Kolb, learning is a social process. It is not simply a matter of digesting information through the receipt of instruction, but is related to what individuals bring with them to the learning situation from their own lived experiences and their ways of responding to new information and new situations. In the context of museums this means that what matters is not simply the knowledge which learners acquire as a consequence of their visit, but also the ways in which they experience and learn during their visit.

The learning process has two dimensions: **apprehension / comprehension** and **extension / intention**. The first dimension defines the way in which a person grasps an experience; the second the way in which a person internalises the experience. Together these two dimensions result in a learning process that is characterised by four different ways of learning. These are: **concrete experience, reflective observation, abstract conceptualisation** and **active experimentation.**

Dreamer: What is the use of this mouse? The visitor is asked to answer this question by using his own imagination. To make an exhibition attractive for a Dreamer, think about the following key words: feeling, personal, creativity, different points of view, poetical, imagination, colour and texture, subjectivity.

Photo: Ivar Pel, University Museum,Utrecht

Deliberator: Here the objects are related to the historical context of the University and the development of Science. This stimulates the visitor to analyze the (chrono)logical relationships of the objects. A Deliberator must be intellectually challenged. Think about the following key words: facts and notions, theory, logical relationship, "the expert is talking", conceptual, background information and beauty, logic and precision.

Photo: Ivar Pel, University Museum, Utrecht

The four ways of learning are related to four different preferred learning styles:

- Concrete experience in combination with reflective observation results in the divergent learning style of people who are **dreamers.**

- Reflective observation in combination with abstract conceptualisation results in the assimilative learning style of people who are **deliberators.**

- Abstract conceptualisation in combination with active experimentation results in the convergent learning style of people who are **deciders.**

- Active experimentation in combination with concrete experience results in the accommodative learning style of people who are **doers.**

Dreamers tend to make use of concrete experience and reflective observation. Their greatest strength lies in their imaginative ability and their awareness of meaning and values. They are able to view concrete situations from many perspectives. The emphasis is on deriving understanding through observation rather than action. Dreamers often perform best in situations that call for the generation of ideas and multiple possibilities, such as 'brainstorming' sessions. Dreamers tend to be interested in people and to be imaginative and in touch with their feelings.

Deliberators tend to make use of abstract conceptualisation and reflective observation. Their greatest strength lies in their ability to assimilate lots of information, to subject the information to reason and analysis, and to arrive at coherent understandings. Deliberators are less focused on people and more concerned with ideas and abstract concepts. Ideas are judged less by their practical value and more by whether they are logically sound and precise.

Deciders tend to make use of abstract conceptualisation and active experimentation. Their greatest strength lies in their ability to get involved in problem solving, decision-making and the practical application of ideas. Deciders often do best in contexts where there is a single correct answer to be found or a solution to a question or problem. In this learning style, knowledge is applied to solving specific problems. Deciders tend to be less emotional as learners. They prefer dealing with technical tasks and problems rather than social and interpersonal issues.

Doers tend to make use of concrete experience and active experimentation. Their greatest strength lies in doing things, in carrying out plans and tasks and getting involved in new experiences. Doers often perform best when there are interesting opportunities, risks and some kind of action to be had. This learning style is best suited for those situations where it is necessary to adapt quickly to changing circumstances. If the theory doesn't fit the plan, doers find it easy to change tack. Problem solving becomes more of an intuitive, trial-and-error process, and relies heavily on other people for information, rather than on their own analytic ability. Doers are usually quite at ease with other people but can be seen as impatient and pushy in a learning situation.

Decider: Put the embryo slides in the right order. The visitor is able to try out theory in practice. For a Decider the exhibition must be: functional, efficient, valid and applicable, using schemes and models, trying out theories, having accompanying materials, rational and practical, technical and problem solving.

Photo: Ivar Pel, University Museum, Utrecht

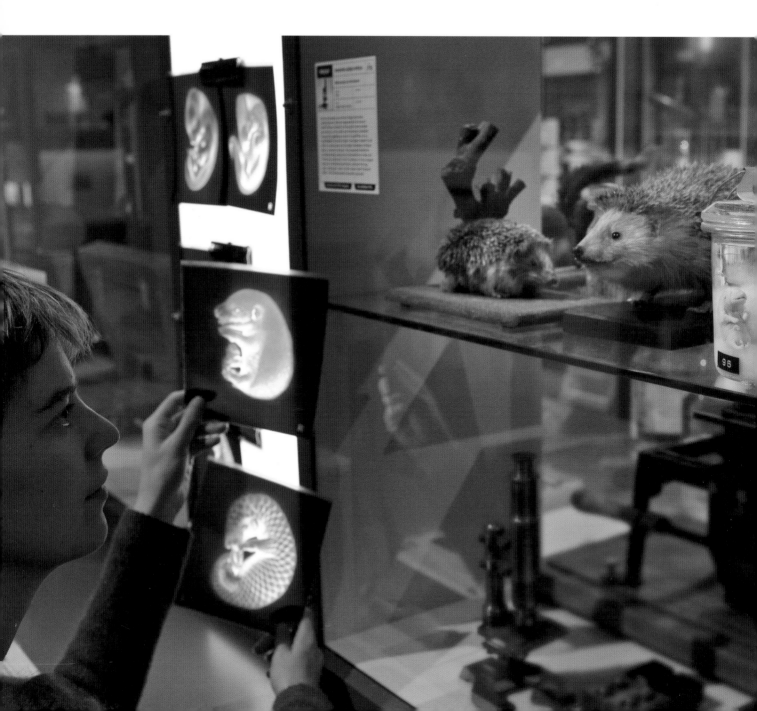

Doer: Jump on this pneumatic pump to find out the force of air. The visitor is actively involved in a way that you can experience by doing. For the Doer an exhibition is about: new experiences, involvement, excitement and variety, competition and risk taking; it must be short and to the point, spectacular, presenting real-life cases and intuitive.

Photo: Ivar Pel, University Museum, Utrecht

KOLB'S LEARNING STYLES IN ACTION IN THE NETHERLANDS

The Kolb project promoted in the Netherlands by the Netherlands Museums Association began by asking what would make an exhibition attractive to those with different learning styles and then translating the characteristics of each style into a checklist that could be used in a museum situation. Each checklist focused on the three key aspects of every exhibition or presentation: content and information, attitude and atmosphere, and design.

The pilot projects led to creative and interesting exhibitions and much discussion about the nature and purpose of learning. But they did meet with some reluctance from members of the project teams. Most educators welcomed the theoretical strengthening of their position and enjoyed inventing approaches and writing texts geared to the different learning styles of visitors. Some designers experienced the learning style theory as a limitation on their creativity. Curators on the whole preferred to stick to their own learning style – mostly that of dreamers or deliberators.

Developing a more rounded approach, one that takes into account the learning diversity of potential visitors, needs time and commitment from the staff involved. But the creation of imaginative approaches to interesting exhibitions, based on the recognition of different learning styles, does go some way to persuading more sceptical colleagues about the value of the approach. If you think there is merit in staging exhibitions that offer learning opportunities for different kinds of learners, the application of Kolb's theories to the organisation of learning may well be worth developing.

Guidelines for applying Kolb's learning theory to exhibition planning:

- Introduce the theory to the full project team, giving case study examples of its success and providing further sources of information. Decide to use it from the very beginning of the new project.

- Encourage all members of the project team to take the Learning Style Test. Use the outcome to decide whether the composition of the team is sufficiently balanced in terms of preferred learning styles. You may need to add others with different learning styles into the team.

- Include someone in the team who is charged with representing the interest of learners, as an audience advocate. The advocate's role is to represent the opinions and voice of the audience and also to make sure that the learning style theory is implemented throughout the project. An audience advocate should be well informed about learning theories in general, the learning style theory in particular, and also with visitor research evidence, both in museums and elsewhere.

- Make sure that provision for each of the four preferred learning styles is built into the design and ground plan of the exhibition. However be aware that an exhibition based on Kolb's learning theory may require additional resources.

To check out the checklist go to www.museumvereniging.nl, "International relations", "Life Long Museum Learning"

For more information about Kolb's learning Style Test and to complete the test online go to www.hayresourcesdirect. haygroup.com

2.4 Identifying learning outcomes

Learning outcomes can be defined as the results of a learning experience. They can apply both to individuals and groups, and may be short-term or long-term. They are generally regarded (in the more formal education sector, at least) as the result of a programme of specific study, and involve judgements being made about individual learner's progress. But learning is a dynamic experience and can be hard to pin down. Some of the most interesting learning outcomes are often those which were not planned or anticipated but which arise in the process of learning and social interaction.

Just as it is quite difficult to apply learning style tests to visitors, so too is it difficult for museums to set specific learning outcomes for learners to achieve. And, given the informality of museum education and the diversity of learning styles, it is not surprising that it is often difficult to measure what has actually been learned. In most cases museums have very little information about the prior knowledge of their visitors. Learning outcomes may often be those described as 'soft' changes in attitudes, values, emotions and beliefs. For those who want 'hard' evidence of demonstrable skills and increased levels of knowledge and understanding, evaluation needs to be carried out or assessment criteria applied.

Compared with formal educational institutions, museums have more difficulties in making judgements about how much their visitors have learned, or how much progress they have made. Useful guidelines and frameworks have been devised for assessing learning, including *Partnerships for Learning: a guide to evaluating arts education projects,* by Felicity Woolf (1999 Arts Council England) and the *Inspiring Learning for All* framework, described below. We should not forget, however, that learners themselves are perfectly capable of making judgements about their own learning. Collecting evidence of learning outcomes in museums, therefore, should be concerned with asking learners about their experience and about what they have learned. We shall look at some ways of doing this in section 3.

In an attempt to describe and then record the impact of all the different types of learning experiences that take place in a museum, the UK Museums Libraries and Archives Council has developed a set of learning outcomes, which should cover all the learning that happens during museum visits. According to this research, what people learn in museums can be categorised within one of five headings:

- **Knowledge and Understanding**
- **Skills**
- **Attitudes and Values**
- **Enjoyment, Inspiration and Creativity**
- **Activity, Behaviour and Progression**

These are called **generic learning outcomes (GLOs),** and can be used both to identify the expected learning outcomes of an educational activity, therefore establishing the ensuing research questions, and to provide the evaluation framework for analysing visitors' responses.

But GLOs only capture people's perceptions of learning. They do not "prove" that that learning has taken place. To do this would mean testing people to see if they really have acquired the knowledge or skills they say they have acquired and museums are never going to be in the business of setting exams to see what their visitors have "learnt", therefore the information available is always going to be highly subjective. However, what people think they have learnt from a museum visit, and what their teachers or parents or group leaders observe about the changes which have taken place as a result of that visit, when collected carefully, analysed systematically, and reported accurately, do enable us to make important observations about the power museums have to inspire and support learning.

Here are some of the most common indicators to aim for when assessing the impact of learning in museum and galleries:

- Increased knowledge of specific subjects

- Enhanced understanding of specific ideas and concepts

- Improved technical and other skills

- A change in attitudes or values

- Evidence of enjoyment, inspiration and creativity

- Evidence of activity, behaviour, progression

- Social interaction and communication

- Increased self-confidence

- Personal development

- Community empowerment

- The development of identity

- Improved health and well-being

www.inspiringlearningforall.gov.uk

(over page) Isolation Cell

Photo: Het Dolhuys Museum, Haarlem

Jean Brady mediating "Come to the edge…"
Photo: Irish Museum of Modern Art, Dublin

Section 3

WAT TE DOEN MET IEMAND DIE SCHOPT OF BIJT OF NAAKT DOOR DE KOU LOOPT, DIE IN ZICHZELF SNIJDT OF ZWAAIT MET EEN MES?

Psychotische mensen zijn niet geweld-dadiger dan anderen. Maar wat te doen met de uitzondering die wél een bedreiging vormt voor zichzelf of zijn omgeving? Vroeger ging hij aan de ketting of in een hok. Of belandde in een dolcel, zoals deze. Dat kon tijdelijk zijn maar ook levenslang – 'patiënten' hadden geen rechten.

Tegenwoordig gelden strenge voor-waarden voor gedwongen opname in een psychiatrische kliniek. Er moet een noodsituatie zijn, zonder alternatief. Hetzelfde geldt voor het gedwongen toedienen van medicijnen.

WEE

3.1 Visitor Research

Visitor research is a way of monitoring, understanding and improving all aspects of learners' and visitors' experiences in museums, from motivations and impressions, to the way they learn from exhibits, and even about snack breaks or use of other facilities. Visitor research can help to identify the intellectual and physical aspects of meeting learners' needs. Interpretation managers and gallery educators use research to become more informed about their audience, and to recognise the dynamics involved in how visitors learn best, so they can devise well-balanced, relevant programmes.

Visitor research and programme evaluation are closely connected. Both assist museum staff to know as much about their visitors and learners as they do about exhibits and objects. Visitor research is not a marketing tool, although it sometimes uses methodologies that are quite similar to market research. Its purpose is to learn more about the characteristics and needs of those who choose to visit museums, so that the resources represented by museums can be deployed more effectively. Research can also be used to determine who does not visit the museum and to suggest ways of attracting them to come.

Visitor research or visitor studies can also be referred to as evaluation. We call it **front-end evaluation,** when done at the initial stage of a project, **formative evaluation**, when conducted at the testing or pilot stage, and **summative evaluation**, when the project is completed.

Greater understanding about who visits museums and why provides useful knowledge which museum curators, interpreters and educators need to acquire when they are planning and developing exhibitions. The study of visitor research also makes clear which groups in the population are not represented in the research findings, and who therefore needs to be the subject of specific outreach activities.

Visitor research establishes a commitment to consultation and dialogue with visitors, in order to respond to their needs and preferences. It involves museum staff wanting to know about their visitors, and potential visitors, and questioning some of their own perceptions and assumptions about how people experience museums and how they learn. It acknowledges that professionals do not know or understand everything about what visitors want. It also assumes that the concept developed is about communicating with an audience and that this communication should be a two-way process. It's an assumption that can be challenging to people working in museums. Instead of believing that the museum experience is a formal, didactic educational model, based on the transmission of knowledge from expert to non-expert, conducting visitor research indicates that the museum and its staff engage in dialogue with their visitors, and develop new projects in co-operation with them.

Visitor research is a useful tool for internal or external advocacy, or for fundraising for a future project. It can draw from previous work and demonstrate how the museum has assessed and learned from mistakes and refocused according to findings. This can give confidence that museum

The Visitor Research Cycle

(Diagram by Juliette Fritsch, Victoria and Albert Museum, London)

This cycle has been developed from the social sciences, predominantly by science museums. It applies scientific methodologies to understanding projects within the museum environment. The visitor research process is iterative.

It is always a good idea to revisit the questions, review the findings, and start the process all over again. Within the Victoria and Albert Museum the cycle is used for gallery development projects, however it can be widely applied.

The first stage of the process is front-end.

This should be done at the stage of initial concept development because it analyses the proposed project from the visitor angle.

It is usually qualitative because it is about exploring motivation, attitude, understanding, perceptions and pre-conceptions about the ideas that the museum is proposing to explore.

The next stage of the process is formative.

This is integral to project design and development and tests prototypes of particular elements of the proposed scheme.

For example, for a gallery project one would test interactives, text hierarchies, tone, presentation, ergonomics, and relationships between objects, cases and orientation.

The final stage is summative.

This happens once the project is up and running, for example, when the exhibition has opened. It's essentially about assessing the effectiveness of the project, and impact on your intended audience.

Summative evaluation is about working out whether or not you've achieved what you set out to achieve.

Meta-evaluation

This can be done at any stage of project development, through surveying other research in the field reading and analysing it to extrapolate the key learning points for your project. This can assist in identifying patterns and trends, and possible quality control criteria. It also identifies areas for development through comparative criteria.

resources will be spent on successful, well thought out projects. As with the findings derived from evaluation studies, conducting visitor research means you should be much more knowledgeable and convincing about your intended audience and better able to justify the proposals you are making.

Visitor research makes it possible to segment museum audiences into a number of different groups. At the Victoria and Albert Museum in London, for example, visitors are divided into the following categories: families, students, schools, professionals in the creative industries, individual adults and groups, with corresponding needs, likes and dislikes.

Detailed knowledge gained from accurate research also helps to inform decision making, not simply in relation to specific projects, but also to support evidence-based policy making and strategic planning within the wider museum.

However, visitor research is costly, both in money and staff time. When it is conducted as formative evaluation, it adds to the time needed for project development. Findings can

challenge colleagues' assumptions about 'the way we always do things'. If the research and evaluation throws up problems, or aspects of the museum's work that are not really very effective, then it implies change and reorganisation in ways that require commitment.

The Victoria and Albert Museum (V&A), one of the largest and most visited national museums in London, conducted detailed visitor research to good effect in the development of the British Galleries, and is now using it in the development of all new exhibitions.

The visitor research used to develop the British Galleries at the V&A involved gallery educators, working with the concept team, to explore different schools of learning theory, in relation to museum visiting. They were able to make good use of several learning style theories to ensure that different kinds of learners could find something relevant for themselves in the design and creation of the galleries.

At the V&A each new exhibition involves a detailed process of concept development, involving gallery curators, interpreters, educators and

audience advocates. Each device in the development of the exhibition is developed with a particular audience and learning style in mind. The whole strategy is informed by visitor research into learning theories and audience segmentation.

3.2 Evaluation

WHAT IS EVALUATION AND WHY DOES IT MATTER?

Evaluation is about gathering evidence to measure the value and quality of the work you are doing, so that you can show:

- **What worked and why**
- **What didn't work and why**
- **What happened in the project**
- **What was provided for those taking part**
- **What difference did it made to individuals, groups, the museum, the wider community**
- **What has been learned by participants, staff, volunteers, partners and the institution**
- **How the money and other resources have been put to good use**
- **What you would do differently next time**

Evaluation involves more than just describing what happened. It's a way of collecting evidence and analysing it so that you can demonstrate to others whether your project met or exceeded your expectations.

Evaluation prompts the educator and the museum to reflect on what has or has not been achieved. It helps to ensure that:

- The project is behaving responsibly towards participants

- Resources are being used effectively

- Learning is taking place in ways which improve, develop and sustain the project.

The evidence gathered during evaluation can be used for advocacy, both inside and outside the museum, for example:

- To convince your organisation to sustain and build on the work

- To support new funding applications for similar work

- To help change and challenge professional and public attitudes

about the value of lifelong learning in museums and galleries.

WHAT SHOULD BE INCLUDED?

Evaluation should relate closely to the aims and needs of the project in question, and to its various stakeholders – participants, project staff, partners, managers, funders and the institution itself. In practice this means information and evidence about:

- The number of people involved in the project as participants

- The work of the project team – roles, meetings held, activities delivered

- Participants' views: what they have learned or liked about the project; how the project has helped them individually, within their families or community and the wider society

- The views of partners and other agencies who had a special interest in the project

- Good practice: what has worked well

- Constraints: areas where the project has faced obstacles or barriers; problems encountered and solutions found

- Impact – how your project has made a difference

- Unexpected outcomes: positive things which happened that hadn't been expected

- Benefits to individuals, groups, museums and communities

- Evidence of value for money.

Evaluation requires the collection of both quantitative and qualitative data.

Quantitative data is statistical: it involves the collecting of figures to show what did or didn't happen. A typical method of quantitative enquiry is a questionnaire with tick box or multiple-choice answers. These are structured and closed-choice responses where the researcher, often the educator or project manager, has already identified the potential data to be covered in answers and structured it before collecting responses. Quantitative work needs to involve a significant percentage of respondents, in order to ensure that the sample size is adequate to support the findings.

In winter

Photo: Terho Aalto, Hameenlinna Art Museum, Hameenlinna

Qualitative data is about capturing and understanding attitudes and ideas. It asks semi-structured and open-ended questions. Qualitative data is gathered in an open way: questions are asked with no prompting for possible answers, and the respondent answers with no guidance from the researcher.

Qualitative work can help to identify potential intellectual barriers and ways of overcoming them. It can also provide the educator with 'quotable quotes' from satisfied participants. Qualitative data may involve a smaller number of respondents than is needed for quantitative data, although the larger the sample size the more representative it will be.

GETTING STARTED
You need to plan and budget for evaluation from the outset. You need to know how you intend to evaluate and what sorts of outcomes you will look for. It's a good idea to have an **evaluation plan** in place at the very beginning of your project, using the five areas below as guidance:

Planning

- Why are you doing this project?

- What specific things do you want to achieve?

- How will you identify success?

Collecting evidence

- How will you collect the evidence you need?

- What methods of collecting evidence will best suit the way you work?

- When – in the lifetime of the project – will you use these methods?

- Who will be involved in giving and collecting the evidence?

Analysing and interpreting the evidence

- What does the evidence tell you?

- Are there any changes you could make in how you are collecting evidence?

Reflecting and moving forward

- What can you learn from the evidence?

- Are there any changes that would improve how the project is working?

- How will you do things differently in the future?

Reporting and sharing

- Who will you tell about the project and why?

- How will you tell them?

- What will you tell them?

WHAT TO WATCH OUT FOR
Projects often get into difficulty when it comes to self-evaluation. Here are some ideas on how to overcome it:

- Planning the evaluation strategy in the initial stages of the project, rather than thinking about it at the last minute

- Defining clear and achievable objectives to be evaluated

- Agreeing who has responsibility for specific areas of data collection and reporting

- Agreeing reporting procedures and developing effective methods of communication

- Operating in an inclusive and participatory way

- Collecting accurate data and interpreting it

- Ensuring that the final report is produced and shared.

CHOOSING METHODS THAT ARE RIGHT FOR YOU

The best record of what your project is achieving comes from a mixture of:

- Ongoing (formative) evaluation and end of project (summative) evaluation

- Quantitative (facts and figures) and qualitative (feelings, experiences, happenings) evidence

- Realistic and appropriate methods that suit the values and size of your organisation.

Facts and figures are essential: for example, how many people are involved, age, gender, origins,

circumstances and needs. Tracking participants through the project provides insight into their development, progression and what happens when they leave. Simple internal monitoring systems to record contact, participation and individual outcomes; all provide evidence about different patterns of engagement over time.

The usual methods for collecting evidence about different people's **experiences** of the project – such as feedback forms, questionnaires and surveys, focus groups, face-to-face and telephone interviews – all provide opportunities for those involved to talk about their experiences in their own words. This means creating and analysing questionnaires, facilitating focus groups and conducting interviews. It also means keeping a record of what people have said.

If you are working with young people, and others who might feel easily daunted by feedback forms, interviews and questionnaires, there are various other ways of collecting evidence that help to capture hopes, experiences and feelings about projects: for example, the use of photo and video-diaries, blogs, graffiti walls and story

boards, music making, creative writing and art work. They rely on activities that are both enjoyable and substantial when it comes to self-expression and learning new skills, but they also provide the vehicle for individuals and groups to express personal, emotional and thoughtful responses to their experiences of the project and to the issues that concern them.

GATHERING THE EVIDENCE

Try to build up as full a picture as possible by gathering different kinds of evidence. For example:

Written and Spoken Evidence

- Check out with participants how they are feeling and what they are learning at regular intervals throughout the project - keep a detailed record or recording of what they say.

- Ask them to write a few things down (anonymously if necessary) which they think you ought to know – including suggestions for changes or improvements.

- Encourage them to do the talking when it comes to making presentations or attending meetings with partners and funders so that a real sense of joint endeavour is obvious.

- Include the words and voices of participants in all communications with the press and in all reports to funders or other agencies.

- Ask partners and providers to give you written feedback from time to time, detailing their perceptions of any strengths and weaknesses.

Visual Evidence

- Keep a photographic record of activities and achievements. Photos can show people doing things and relating to each other, as well as providing a record of events and special occasions. Make sure that any photos are on display to reinforce group solidarity and a sense of belonging.

- The use of video and DVD cameras to record activities not only helps develop technical and creative skills, the results can be useful for presentation purposes.

- If words get in the way, ask participants to paint their feelings on large sheets of paper at various stages of the project. It can be fun and is a way of also getting them talking about what they have experienced.

3.3 Teamwork

N.B. In Dutch the word "presentation" as applied to museums refers to exhibition planning with an educational input or element

Exhibitions in museums have traditionally reflected the viewpoint of the curator, translated into a 'public friendly' exhibition by the designer. In many cases the influence of those who are knowledgeable in learning and learning styles (educators, presentation staff, cultural mediators and interpretation staff) is peripheral, as their role is to write explanatory text or devise education programmes once the overall concept and content have been decided, without being able to influence it from the beginning.

To ensure that an exhibition is able to reach as many people as possible – whether as an aesthetic, scientific, historical or other experience – it is of vital importance to give those in the museum who are specialists in the field of learning a position of influence in the project team, as an audience advocate or as the manager of the project team. This is what happens at the Maritime Museum in Rotterdam.

At the Maritime Museum in Rotterdam the creation of exhibitions is no longer managed by curators but by a member of the presentation department, which brings together educators and project managers (specialists in displays and exhibitions). Although the role of project manager has been fairly common in the Netherlands for some time, this has added an important dimension by combining project management with interpretation.

The process at the Maritime Museum starts with an idea. Anyone, inside or outside the museum, can submit a proposal for an exhibition. The management team (in which all heads of departments are represented) makes an initial selection of ideas for projects and sends them to the presentation advice committee, which has members from various disciplines: presentation, education, research and marketing and communications. The committee members assess proposals on the basis of their own professional expertise before making a joint recommendation. On the basis of their advice, the management team then decides which ideas shall be realised as exhibitions.

Once the programming has been established, the management team appoints a project manager. He/she is directly responsible to the management team, which means that exhibition projects are set up outside the usual line-management hierarchies. Project managers are able to act decisively and to work efficiently but everything they do is dependent on good teamwork.

Project groups are made up of colleagues with different professional disciplines. The project manager has two important tasks: the interpretation of the content of an exhibition (how to tell a story and for whom) and leading the project group. The curator carries out research, recommends museum objects and writes the texts used in the exhibition. The project manager and the curator, together with the exhibition designer, work intensively together from the start of a project on the development and detailing of the exhibition. The involvement of the educator ensures that educational criteria inform the exhibition's design. Educator and project manager together devise the interpretive techniques– for example, hands-on exhibits, interactive exhibits, computer programmes,

film, audio, evocative exhibits etc. – and work out the respective details. The head of the technical services department is brought into the picture when the first design is presented. The project secretary keeps a record of all meetings and loans from external organisations. The marketing and communications assistant is responsible for ensuring that the intended target groups are contacted as effectively as possible. The marketing and communications department is responsible for 'selling' the exhibition and is assigned its own budget for this purpose.

During the entire process, which takes about a year on average, the project group meets at least five times to make decisions and share information. The day-to-day work is carried out by members of the team working together on the interpretation methods, the educational programme, layout and lighting plans, promotion, loaned objects, a text plan, an event programme and the opening. The project is closed with an evaluation.

The Maritime Museum Rotterdam has built up years of experience of working in this way. In the process, working

practices have evolved which make a vital contribution to the educationally rich, well thought out and attractive final result. By thinking carefully about target groups and interpretive techniques and by involving all the necessary people at an early stage in the process, the museum is able to achieve a well-balanced exhibition, in which education and the transfer of information are integral components of the whole presentation.

NOTES FROM THE DIARY OF THE PROJECT MANAGER
'Dozens of round-bosomed women staring out at us *(over page),* gilded mast tops reaching into the sky, man-sized figureheads and fearsome lions... I am standing with a curator in the stores of the Maritime Museum Rotterdam and I am about to embark on an assignment that the management team has given us: prepare an exhibition about ship decorations that should not only be about individual objects, but also the historical stories and with plenty of room for anecdotes. After brainstorming and talking together at length, we have come up with an interesting perspective for our story: why do people decorate their ships?

There are four possible answers to this question:

- **to show who you are**
- **to protect yourself from evil**
- **to show how rich and powerful you are**
- **to show how beautiful you are**

We have found a basis for our story and can develop four themes for the exhibition: identity, superstition/belief, power and beauty. The themes are also a fairly accurate reflection of modern society. Objects with a decorative or ornamental function are, after all, timeless - even though young people today prefer to say 'blings' and 'glams'. But it does not matter if you are decorating a ship or wearing designer clothes - it's all about showing who you are! This principle will also be used as a basis for the communication plan, which will start with an evocative title: *STEM TO STERN – ship's decoration from bow to stern*. We've made a start....!'

RECOMMENDATIONS FOR PROJECT MANAGERS

- Make sure you have the support of museum managers and keep the whole organisation well informed about the progress of the project

- Have a plan and a schedule. Don't let important deadlines slip

- Good communication within the project team is vital. Make it a priority

- Lead with a positive attitude and continue to inspire and motivate project team members

- Designers all have their own style. Change the designer if you want variation

- Plan project group meetings to coincide with important steps in the exhibition process

- Take stock of how you are doing as you go along. Make any adjustments and changes before it is too late

- Make meetings efficient and short. Make sure the necessary people are present. Communicate any decisions to the wider project team

- Evaluate the process as well as the product. What have you learned? What will you do differently next time?

3.4 Partnership

Successful organisations tend to be those which are outward-looking with a positive approach to partnership working. This is because partnerships, if developed effectively, can bring enormous benefits. They allow organisations to:

- Access skills and experience which they do not have in house

- Explore different ways of delivering services

- Pool resources and maximise investment

- Develop the skills base of their staff

- Find new outlets for their goods and services

- Make savings through joint procurement and delivery

- Share expertise and ideas

- Punch above their weight by acting in concert

- Develop a more attractive offer to potential users.

'Dozens of round-bosomed women staring at us.'
Photo: Fred Ernst, Maritime Museum, Rotterdam

What special exhibits should be used and for what purpose? A model ship is created with decorations and built-in lights that visitors can switch on and off. This allows them to discover the location of different types of ship decoration

Photo: Fred Ernst, Maritime Museum, Rotterdam

The 'special' of a ship's bow, inspired by well-known images from the film Titanic, is designed
to make visitors think about their own identity: what kind of figurehead would I choose to be?
Visitors can choose a figurehead on the touch screen and see their own face appear in the picture.
They can take a photo of themselves as a figurehead, which they can also e-mail to a friend.

Photo: Fred Ernst, Maritime Museum, Rotterdam

Creating the exhibition shows how important it is to involve an educator from the very beginning. Because 'decoration' as a topic links up well with youth culture and various vocational educational targets, it is decided to develop a workshop as part of the programme where visitors can see how ship decorations are made.

Photo: Fred Ernst, Maritime Museum, Rotterdam

The designers are briefed about the proposed atmosphere of the exhibition and come up with an idea: water is the element which binds the themes together, and also acts as a necessary barrier to protect valuable figureheads and ornaments. Pieces of glass illuminated with blue light appear to shine and sparkle like water. For safety reasons, the glass will have to be covered over. A solution is found by using perforated metal sheets that can be laid over the glass.

Photo: Fred Ernst, Maritime Museum, Rotterdam

Museums which are keen to work with a broad range of audiences, and in particular with hard to reach and excluded groups, should build up effective partnerships with youth and other social services, faith groups, voluntary organisations, health care organisations, arts practitioners and local businesses, to name but a few examples. Evaluation reports of museum services should demonstrate the range and breadth of the partnerships the museum has formed, and how these add value to the museum offer.

Partnership is critical to all aspects of a museum's work and is especially important for museum educators trying to make contact with a wide cross section of people. In any one year a museum education service might be working with formal and informal education providers, adult learners, refugees and asylum seekers, cultural minorities, teachers, community groups, pensioners, children with special educational needs, teenagers, single mothers, librarians, archivists, people with disabilities or mental health difficulties. No single education department can employ enough experienced staff to develop and run

the range and type of programmes all these different groups need.

This is where partnership comes into its own, by offering specialist knowledge and contact with potential audiences. Good practice always involves developing working relationships with representatives and users themselves from non-traditional groups to help inform and shape the work which is being developed.

The UK Museums Libraries and Archives Council's (MLA) best practice framework, Inspiring Learning for All (ILFA), sees partnership as critical to developing and delivering high quality learning experiences for users and provides a checklist and guidance on developing and maintaining effective partnerships.

The framework starts from the premise that partnerships can only succeed where time is invested in:

- Researching and investigating potential partners

- Understanding their perspectives and needs and seeing how far these align with your own

- Establishing the outcomes which the partnership will deliver

- Establishing clear guidance for how you will work together

- Agreeing roles and responsibilities

- Making sure you have adequate resources to support the work

- Training staff to work together and to share and develop their skills

- Allowing for regular sharing of information and ideas, progress reports, and evaluation.

Not all partnerships should go on forever. Some will, and should be, time limited – designed to deliver a certain set of outcomes and capable of moving on to a different phase once these have been accomplished.

The ILFA framework provides a check list for organisations to use in order to understand both where they are in terms of partnership based working and guidance on how to make partnerships more effective. The guidance is based on the best practice which emerged from initial piloting.

Key questions for organisations to consider as they review their services, or start to think about developing new ones, include:

- Do you identify suitable partners and evaluate the benefits of working in partnership to support learning?

- Do you work with partners to plan and develop learning opportunities?

- Do you invite contributions from outside the museum to broaden the range and appeal of learning opportunities?

In relation to each of these areas ILFA then asks a further series of questions designed to encourage museums to explore in more detail whether they are following best practice in terms of developing and maintaining partnerships, how they know they are doing this and how they might demonstrate it to others.

Some examples of relevant questions are:
Have you …

- Identified a range of partners with whom you might work effectively?

- Identified how the work of partner organisations will add value to your own work?

- Reviewed, recorded and re-enforced the benefits of working with partners and the lessons learned?

- Strategies in place for partners to give their views on the relevance and impact of services

- Acted on decisions to withdraw from unproductive partnerships?

- Secured additional funding for partnership working

- Identified ways of pooling resources, skills and experiences

- Used your skills, resources and collections to add value to others learning initiatives?

Do you know whether…

- Staff can describe the benefits of partnership working in developing their own skills?

- Staff have participated in information and skills exchanges to widen understanding and share good practice?

- Partners are satisfied with working arrangements and your contribution to projects?

- Partners can say what they have gained from working with you?

- Users have benefited from your partnership programmes?

ILFA is based on the premise that organisations need to be more reflective about what they do; that they should be learning organisations themselves as well as organisations which stimulate and support other people's learning. Working in partnership with others is part of this process, opening doors for staff to challenge and consider their own ways of working and to share knowledge, skills and experience with others.

ILFA:
www.inspiringlearningforall.gov.uk

3.5 Outreach

Outreach is the term most often used to describe making contact with groups that do not routinely visit museums and galleries, because of economic status, social exclusion, lack of confidence, educational and institutional barriers or general alienation from museums as relevant cultural institutions. The implication of making cultural rights a central part of how you think about what you do, is that provision should be made available to a much wider and more diverse audience of visitors than currently participate in what museums and galleries have to offer.

In practice the concept outreach has a number of related meanings and uses. It can mean:

- Liaising and making contact with community-based organisations and groups.

- Raising awareness of existing museum services and learning opportunities.

- Widening participation and access to museums and museum learning by engaging groups identified as economically, socially and/or educationally disadvantaged.

- Working in informal and participative ways with people outside the museum.

- Mounting exhibitions and learning opportunities in community locations.

- Developing new exhibitions and learning programmes in response to the identified need.

- Assisting community groups in developing their own exhibitions.

- Providing community-based learning activities as a stepping stone to museum-based mainstream programmes.

- Training local people as volunteers, guides, interpreters, audience advocates.

Museum outreach can be based on different models. For example:

- **Satellite** – establishing exhibitions and learning activities in fixed community locations.

- **Peripatetic** – delivering museum activities in various organisational settings such as hostels, day centres, homes for the elderly, hospitals, prisons.

- **Detached outreach** – contacting people outside of organisational settings e.g. in streets, shopping centres, bars, at the school gates.

- **Domiciliary outreach** – visiting people in their own homes.

- **Distance learning** – providing on-line services for people in rural and isolated locations or who are house-bound because of physical impairments or disabilities.

All of these are best used in partnership with educational outreach workers and exiting organisations that have strong roots in community settings.

In order to conduct outreach work effectively, three essential ingredients are necessary:

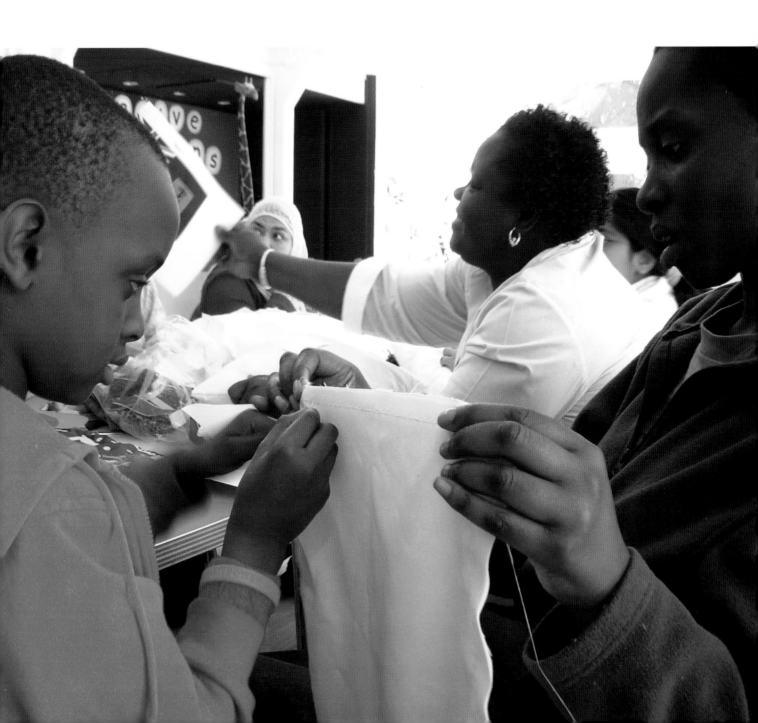

- **Organisational support and commitment.** The full commitment and support of board and senior management is essential for the museum to position itself as a social institution with outreach as one of its vital roles.

- **Adequate resources.** Outreach should be supported by both short-term and more permanent funding – the first to permit experimentation and innovation; the second to allow museums to build established and sustained relationships in communities where their presence can have a long term impact.

- **The right staff with the right skills:** Outreach workers have to accomplish a number of complex tasks which require a range of practical and interpersonal skills. These may be less to do with qualifications than with personal characteristics such as good communication and listening skills. The effectiveness of any outreach endeavour ultimately depends on the web of relationships which workers are able to establish in the community. Those involved in outreach are more likely to be accepted when they have backgrounds and characteristics similar to those of the target groups.

At the initial stage, outreach staff may need to:

- Conduct local research and analyse the resulting data

- Identify local networks and individuals

- Contact and negotiate with a range of different agencies, groups and individuals at both official and grassroots levels

- Develop partnerships with local agencies and other organisations

- Organise and administer meetings with disparate groups and organisations

- Engage people, as individuals or in groups, in dialogue about their interests and priorities

- Offer information, advice and guidance on available opportunities and resources held at the museum

- Identify learning interests and needs and devise appropriate ways of meeting them

- Broker activities between groups and the museum

- Locate and negotiate the use of detached premises for museum purposes.

At the exhibition or programme delivery stage, outreach staff may need to:

- Work with museum colleagues to organise activities in response to identified needs

- Facilitate activities

- Find resources to provide necessary support for participants – such as transport costs, child-care, support for people with disabilities

- Evaluate progress and outcomes

- Monitor and evaluate the work and produce written reports.

Outreach workers need to have sensitivity; respect for others and the host communities; the ability to listen and to convert what they hear into constructive activity; the ability to adapt to different groups and different situations and to react to widely differing wants and needs. They also need to be able to work autonomously, sometimes in isolation, and to handle conflict.

Staff development and training is essential to support outreach staff in their work, but also to enable museum-based staff to benefit from the knowledge and expertise of outreach staff when they are asked to respond to non-traditional audiences in museum and other settings.

CASE STUDY: EMPOWERING THE LOCAL COMMUNITY

The Nature Museum (Natuurmuseum) in Tilburg, the Netherlands, has as its aim to advance the knowledge and the appreciation of nature, especially in regard to the human being and his or her natural and cultural habitat. In this context the museum supports the development of exhibitions in local communities, organised by the residents themselves.

The museum offers organisational support, and lends showcases and objects from the collection. The local community itself chooses the subject of the exhibition.

One such exhibition was 'A Park in Waspik', about the reconstruction of a city park in Waspik, a community of the city of Waalwijk. The exhibition consisted of two elements:

- the history of the location (based on research done by the inhabitants)

- the flora and fauna in the park (with loans from the museum).

All of the outreach projects in the exhibition were held on location in the central hall of the community centre of Waspik. The exhibition resulted in a greater involvement by the local community in the planning of the new city park, which also got its new name from the exhibition: Park Waspik.

CASE STUDY: A VIRTUAL OUTREACH PROJECT

The website 'The memory of Oost' (a quarter in Amsterdam where many immigrants live), is the initiative of the Amsterdam Historical Museum. The website has been created with the support of many organisations and individuals living and working in Oost. The idea of the website is to combine all kinds of photographs and stories relating to Oost. Many of the stories were set up as interviews in which locals interviewed each other. Hundreds of stories were the result. The people involved were invited to special visits to the museum in the centre of Amsterdam. The links

between the museum and the local community are still strong, three years after the start of the project. The close partnership has resulted in cultural objects associated with the newcomers becoming acquisitions for the museum, where they have formed the basis for a new kind of exhibition. One of these, 'My Veil' (2006), was about the different ways in which veils are worn by Muslim women. The exhibition attracted much attention both from both 'old' and 'new' Amsterdammers.

Amsterdam Historical Museum: www.geheugenvanoost.nl.

(over page) Photo: Sue Parkins, NIACE

Section 4

Developing educational activities addressed to adults in museums means changing perspectives, carrying out audience research, consulting with the participants, and addressing new visitors. Throughout this process staff and the museum must be open to change and willing to be challenged by innovative projects. In some new contexts, museum educators working with adult audiences say they often feel like learners themselves because of the significance attached to involving participants, and the high degree of creative thinking and innovation that such initiatives entail.

In this section, we present examples of projects developed by museums and addressed to adults, which demonstrate aspects of good practice in a variety of settings. While by no means exhaustive, they offer some insight into the work which can be done with adults in museums, drawing on the expertise of museum practitioners across Europe. We have not been able to include all types of adult learning programmes here, and you may find that a particular interest of yours has not been included. But for further case studies and examples,

please see the resources section at the back of this publication, especially the Collect & Share website, which contains case studies searchable by a number of criteria including type of group and country

www.collectandshare.eu.com.

4.1 Family Learning

WHAT IS MEANT BY FAMILY LEARNING?

Family learning in museums defines the family as any group of people of different generations who arrive together in the museum accompanied by at least one child. The definition is not confined to parents and their children, or to groups related by bloodline, or even marriage, but to any multi-generational group. The definition excludes school groups, because they come to engage in a more formal type of learning. It also excludes couples and other all-adult family groups because they tend to behave as groups of adults, and

behave quite differently from those visiting with children.

HOW IMPORTANT ARE FAMILY LEARNERS TO MUSEUMS?

A survey among the museums of the Dutch province of Gelderland (2002) showed that 25% of the visitors came with children under the age of 12. This was an average – in some museums it was even 30%, 50% and, in one natural history museum, even 74%. One-third of these visitors came from the neighbourhood.

A recent Italian survey provides some useful data. The Fondazione Fitzcarraldo surveyed museum visitors in Lombardy in March 2004 and found that 24.2% of their sample visited with their own children or with nieces and nephews, and a further 11.6% visited with relatives. They estimated that overall, 25 - 30 % of the museum audience in the region of Lombardy consisted of family groups. In some contexts the percentage was even higher. At the Museo della Storia Naturale in Milan, for example, some 40% of visitors arrived in family groups.

At roughly the same time as the Lombardy survey, the Museums

Libraries and Archives Council in Britain asked MORI to do a survey based on a sample of the whole of the UK population, not just museum visitors, looking at among other things their museum visiting habits. Of this sample 32% said they visited museums in families. Those less affluent groups, who do not usually visit museums, were far more likely to visit if they had children or grandchildren, and 45% of those with children said they were interested in science and technology.

These few examples do not of course tell the whole story but they do show that inter-generational groups form around a quarter to a third of museum visitors, in the Netherlands, Italy and the UK. This represents a very important proportion of museum visitors indeed, and is even more significant for museums of science and natural science.

WHAT ARE THE PARTICULAR NEEDS OF FAMILY GROUPS?

In the mid 1990s Harris Qualitative was commissioned to investigate the needs and attitudes of children and their accompanying parents when visiting museums and other places of interest. Their work, published in 1997, *Children as an audience for Museums and Galleries,* is based on qualitative, in-depth focus group discussion with children and their carers.

They found that families usually went out together on holidays and at weekends: sometimes children were motivated by following up school visits, but both adults and children were drawn to big themes or links with television programmes.

To attract families to museums the expectation that the visit will be fun is crucial. The main success factor seems to be the provision of things to do. Tactile experiences, drawing and making things, historical enactment and dramatic performance, computer-based activities, effective interactives and experiments are all cited as important motivating factors that encourage families to visit. Amazing buildings and fascinating objects are great draws and taking home a souvenir is usually part of the pleasure.

HOW DO FAMILY GROUPS LEARN?

Surveys such as the MORI in the UK indicate that all parents, from all academic or socio-economic groups, regard museums as important places for children's learning, whether they used them themselves or not.

Family groups go to museums to find things out together, as a way of spending time with each other and doing something educational. This type of learning is often described as social, or collaborative, learning. It cements family relationships and relies on interaction among members. The family members spend time in conversation, sharing what they know and what they find out. They talk about what they already know. The adults have a strong tendency to reinforce past experiences and family history to develop a shared understanding among family members. Their discussion tends to be close and personal, in that they talk about the exhibits and use the labels, even reading them together, sometimes out loud.

Sometimes conversation is less important than observing each other, and modelling each other's behaviour, on the use of an interactive device, for example. Some intergenerational groups, especially those with older children, rely on modelling, splitting up for periods and only coming together to talk occasionally. This demonstrates more independent forms of learning.

From the catalogue of the exhibition Gli occhi del pubblico (Bologna, IBC-CLUEB, 2006)

Photo: Paolo Righi

What emerges from research is that the adults in the group facilitate the children's learning. Families have a culture of shared knowledge and the museum visit enriches their store of knowledge. Their conversations and discussion begin with prior knowledge and continue after their visit. The museum becomes an important part of the family learning experience.

It makes sense therefore that when adults feel at home in a museum, and interested in its exhibits, they are more likely to transmit these feelings to the children and the family will learn more as a result. Adults like to be offered activity kits or interactive exhibits and to feel confident in using them. When they do, they appear to facilitate deeper levels of learning.

These emerging findings are important as many museums are now investing in the provision of learning materials, aimed at giving adults visiting with children the means to facilitate group learning.

WHAT CAN MUSEUMS DO TO ATTRACT AND RETAIN VISITORS IN FAMILY GROUPS?

Good practice involves:

- Knowing what families would like to learn and taking this into account in the design of exhibitions. Museums can't afford to ignore the requirements of so many of their visitors.

- Providing special activities and events for family groups, particularly on the weekends and during the school holidays. Family learning in museums is adult-led but child-oriented. Adults must feel able to make use of the available resources to guide and stimulate the interest of their children. No other groups learn in this way and the numbers involved merit special attention and investment.

- Offering families attractive prices for entrance costs, education packs or activity kits, and special events and workshops. Is the restaurant or café 'family friendly'? Does it offer a selection of reasonably-priced food which children will want to eat?

- Becoming more welcoming. Museums should encourage social interaction, be relaxed about noise and provide space to move freely, sit down, and even to eat a packed lunch or feed the baby.

- Providing intelligent and entertaining things to do. Wherever possible, interactive devices should be designed so that people can share the experience, and adults can guide children. Computers are always in demand but activities need to provide enough space for several people to gather round and look together. It is unlikely that family groups will be attracted by rows of glass cases.

- Investing in learning materials for adults to use with children. Kits and packs offer families independence to learn together by suggesting activities, games and trails, and often doubling as things to take home. Even a simple list of follow up questions to take home could deepen a family's learning experience by stimulating further discussion about an exhibition or a series of objects.

- Providing knowledgeable and friendly front-line staff and special demonstrators to interact with families if they choose to take part. But some care is needed here. It may not suit all families to have too many professionals getting in the way of their own social interaction with their children. There are some excellent examples of manned object trolleys, storytelling, and roleplay sessions, whereby skilled museum workers engage young visitors with their carers, but this usually takes the place of parental facilitation. More research is needed to identify the particular needs of families in these types of interactions.

- Providing high quality labelling, with different levels and complexities of information: from the simple to the more in-depth. Label trails, whereby children answer questions or find items or objects by reading the label help families and everyone else to enjoy the visit and appreciate the work more – as well as learning together. Labels should be written avoiding the use of museum jargon which only people who work in museums understand or need to know.

4.2 Young People

Younger children enjoy visiting museums, both as part of a school group and with families or other adults. However young adults or 'young people' (aged between 14 and 25) show a sharp decline in museum-going: they are likely to be the least represented age group in the museum, except where there are programmes particularly addressed to their needs. They often feel that museums are not for them; they think of museums as places for younger or older visitors; and they often feel socially or intellectually intimidated by exhibits or works of art, or even from entering the building in the first place.

GOOD PRACTICE IN WORKING WITH YOUNG PEOPLE BASED ON THE ENVISION RESEARCH PROJECT

The Envision research project, co-ordinated by Engage (UK 2002 - present), came about as a result of significant research reports highlighting young people's lack of involvement in cultural activity, the lack of meaningful opportunities for young people in art museums, the value of such activities in personal, social and educational terms to young people where they did exist (in particular to young people experiencing or at risk of social exclusion because of a lack of access to education, training or employment), and the lack of skills, expertise and understanding of young people within the arts, cultural and heritage sector. Envision was set up to support the gallery sector to develop a culture of participation amongst young people outside of the formal education system, in particular benefiting those young people who are believed to be disadvantaged, experiencing or at risk of social exclusion.

Among the questions which the project has addressed are:

- How can museums engage young people ages 14-21 – particularly those outside of formal education?

- What are the challenges and the benefits to the educator and the cultural institution of involving young people – including those from so-called 'disadvantaged' backgrounds?

Envision aims to do more than simply run one-off projects or attract new audiences: working with a wide range of young people outside of formal education, the first phase of envision promoted an action-research approach which required project leaders and partners to set out questions which they wished to investigate, and encouraged risk-taking in how they did this. Envision seeks to find sustainable ways of involving young people in organisational review, consultation

From the catalogue of the exhibition Gli occhi del pubblico (Bologna, IBC-CLUEB, 2006)

Photo: Tano d'Amico

and decision-making to embed a 'youth-friendly' ethos at the heart of the institution. A distinctive feature of envision is that it sets out to do more than involve young people in creative opportunities, but also to support young people to influence and shape cultural provision, creating genuine benefits and relevance to their lives. The second phase of envision, due to begin in 2007, will focus on training, advice and support for projects in sixteen venues, helping more cultural organisations to work with young people by developing facilities and provision with a 'youth-friendly' face, and by reviewing organisational culture to commit to working with young people.

The first phase of the envision research project involved eight art museums working in partnership with youth agencies and professional artists. They collaborated with 150 'hard to reach' young people ages 14-21 from outside of formal mainstream education. The young people were recruited from youth clubs, volunteer agencies, social and health services, sheltered accommodation, local colleges, pupil referral units, school and neighbourhood drop-in centres.

A quick overview of three of the projects will give an idea of the scope of envision:

- **Connect 4** at the Royal Pump Rooms, Leamington Spa, sought to find out how galleries can overcome barriers to participation by young people and build long-term relationships within rural networks. The venue initially planned to develop sustained partnerships with local youth centres, engaging young people in consultation about gallery development leading to a young people's exhibition which would be toured around local villages in a mobile bus. The final project was re-planned following difficulties in establishing the partnerships which had originally been envisaged. A strong partnership with a local skate club was formed and rather than curate an exhibition to be toured around local villages, the group worked with an artist and designer to create their own website magazine highlighting local cultural places and opportunities for young people, essentially citing the Royal Pump Rooms within young people's local cultural networks.

Visit the site at www.subcultures.org.

- **Sample Arts** at Ikon, Birmingham, wanted to find out how they could work with a partner youth organisation to devise an effective process of working with contemporary visual arts to engage and enhance the lives and skills of young people. A two-phase project was devised: in the first phase a series of training and skill-sharing sessions took place for museum staff (education team and visitor assistants), artists, youth workers and young people enabling everyone to have a voice, communicate on an equal basis and share skills, ideas and understanding of each other's culture and expertise. Through practical workshops and facilitated discussions, young people, staff and youth workers developed technical, personal and social skills, explored the exhibition programme and also the venue itself. In the second phase the venue plans to create an interactive website targeted at youth workers and young people. The website will aim to be an ongoing tool to disseminate information and share good practice with other young people, cultural organisations and service providers.

The K 9 Card

Photo: Terho Aalto, Hameenlinna Art Museum, Hameenlinna

- **Creative Consultants** at Manchester Art Gallery investigated how art museums can become more inclusive of young people, not just in the education departments, but also across the whole service. Through 'creative consultancy' young people engaged in an audit of Manchester Art Gallery's work and produced a video report making recommendations to staff. The young people then worked alongside the gallery team across different departments to curate a high-profile exhibition called 'Disguise' aimed at audiences 16-25 years old. A report produced as part of this project has informed future strategy for the inclusion of young people at Manchester Art Gallery, and the Creative Consultants group has continued to grow and has been involved in delivering a wide range of projects and events at venue.

GOOD PRACTICE GUIDELINES
Creating a youth-friendly organisational culture

- Strong management support is crucial, both for organisational learning and change to take place. Build this into project activities, either through direct managerial involvement in the project or through presentations to senior management at key intervals.

- Involve colleagues and partners at all stages of project planning, delivery and follow-up for the widest possible organisational impact. Give staff a role to play – including staff who don't usually come into contact with young people in the course of their work and staff who may have negative ideas about young people.

- Involve staff from across the organisation in training and planning to challenge current practice and develop a shared mission.

Tackling barriers to young people's participation in museums:

- Identify barriers during the planning stage. For example, is it the image of the organisation, staff skills / attitudes, lack of contact with young people or youth agencies, relevance of the programme or the space available to work with young people? Identifying the barriers will help you to devise strategies to overcome these. Some barriers will be relatively easy to overcome (for example basic comfort – refreshments, comfortable working area, welcoming greeting to the participants); some will be more deeply entrenched within the organisation and may take much longer to address.

- Ask and involve young people and also the 'gatekeepers' (those who work with young people or who are within their sphere of influence) at an early stage and throughout the project.

- Ensure that all staff are fully briefed, youth-friendly and do not jeopardize the project. Remember to involve front of house staff.

Sustainability and legacy – what to do when the project has finished?

- Build legacy and a strategy for sustainability into the planning process, and be ready for new opportunities to occur during the project stage. This might include new organisational policies, increased commitment to young people or a young people's steering / consultation group.

- Dialogue with young people may be sustained via newsletters, website, further partnerships, invitation to museum events / openings, or a volunteer programme.

From the catalogue of the exhibition Gli occhi del pubblico (Bologna, IBC-CLUEB, 2006)
Photo: Isabella Balena

- Links with youth agencies made during the project can offer additional opportunities and support to young people after the project has finished.

4.3 Older Learners

In this publication we are defining 'older' people as anyone over the age of retirement – depending on which country, this might be 60, 65 or 70 years old. Thus older visitors include both healthy, active and recently retired persons as well as more elderly and possibly more frail members of the community.

Older and more frequent museum visitors are often from well educated social groups. They are likely to be familiar with museums and to feel comfortable in the surroundings. They may need to be pointed in the direction of educational activities aimed at people with more leisure time, which they did not have time for during their working lives. They often become enthusiastic life long learners, even when they are new to museum education.

Older people without the benefits of good education and resources, however, may feel less at home in museums. Some might have mobility problems and feel deterred by crowds and public transport. Museums as institutions may have a negative image, appear tiring, be associated with learned people, seem difficult to reach, feel uninviting, have texts that are difficult to read and high entrance fees. Museums that want to attract older, culturally inexperienced visitors need to devise programmes which take account of their needs.

This means providing enough rest stops, easy access, texts that are easily readable in terms of print size and positioning. Programmes should provide social contact. Successful programmes with older learners have included nostalgia, anecdotes or reminiscence, demonstrations, living history, historic art, ceramics, local history, local costumes, and handicraft. It is important not to stereotype older learners or to assume they will not be interested in projects concerning modern or contemporary themes, as this example from the Irish Museum of Modern Art demonstrates.

WORKING WITH OLDER ADULTS AND CONTEMPORARY ART

Early in 1991, as the Irish Museum of Modern Art in Dublin (IMMA) was preparing to open to the public, a close working relationship was established with the St. Michael's Parish Active Retirement Association. This was in keeping with the Museum's intended policy of involving the local community in the life and work of the Museum. It also recognised the potential and role of older people in contemporary visual culture. A group of older residents from the nearby area of Inchicore in Dublin had formed their Association at local level as part of a nationwide network of voluntary groups.

THE PROGRAMME

The work with older learners - as with all the education programmes at IMMA - is an active learning experience, involving three elements of art education: making art; meeting artists and discussing with them the conceptual basis of their work; and looking at and responding to artworks in the museum's temporary exhibitions and permanent collection.

Practical workshops take place in the museum's studios. In the workshops the group involved is able to explore a range of art materials, tools and techniques; explore their own ideas, values and interests to create work themselves; and benefit from the advice and teaching of artists who help them move from an idea to a finished piece of work

Each element provides a different perspective from which to view and engage with artworks and the world in which art objects are created.

In the early stages of a programme with older adults it is often necessary to introduce basic art making skills, using a broad range of art processes. It is essential to make time for 'learning and un-learning'. Schooling might have been a negative experience for some participants so they need time to build up confidence and develop new skills.

OLDER ADULTS AS CURATORS

In 1998, an invitation was extended to the St. Michael's group to curate an exhibition from the Museum's Permanent Collection, In preparation for this exhibition, entitled, 'Come to the Edge', the group of older

learners worked with museum staff on questions of interpretation.

Every week for three months the group of older learners worked with two artists in a series of practical workshops, exploring artworks from the Museum's permanent collection, using the same principles outlined above. They made their own responses to selected artworks, focusing on responses that the work evoked for them.

Then they worked with the Senior Curator of the Collection and the Educator / Curator to develop an understanding of the curatorial process, i.e. the identification of exhibition themes and the selection of individual works from the Collection to illustrate the chosen themes. They also observed a group of teenagers curating a show from the collection – called 'Somebodies' - and met and exchanged learning with them.

Through a series of weekly meetings, discussions, tours of the exhibitions on display and slide shows of works in storage, the members of the group explored ideas relating to collections and collecting policies,

acquisitions and donations, exhibitions and exhibition-making. They then researched, selected and took part in the installation of the exhibition as well as researching and writing the wall texts and catalogue.

OLDER PEOPLE AS MEDIATORS

Older people regularly facilitate tours of both their own work and in the case above of the 'Come to the Edge' exhibition at IMMA. This respects their role as advocates and champions, in ways that help to draw new audiences to the Museum. The group members find the experience interesting and challenging and require the Museum to continue to find ways to support them and keep them involved in such activities.

OLDER PEOPLE AS KEYWORKERS

Older people are also encouraged to become keyworkers or hosts at the Museum in a variety of ways that complement the role of the full time Museum staff. They are encouraged to contribute to conferences, thus developing their role beyond the gallery or studio. And as hosts to other older people's groups visiting the

Museum they are a valuable ingredient in a growing network. They also input to the Museum's National Programme which lends artworks from its Collection in co-curated exhibitions throughout Ireland. Education initiatives are programmed in each location.

The key points arising from the work with older learners at IMMA are:

- Projects need to be well structured with plenty of time for development.

- Budgeting needs to be realistic.

- The programme has evolved slowly, always taking its cue from the older people themselves and pacing the new elements in accordance with the participants needs or stated wishes.

- Ongoing evaluation takes place through group discussion at the end of each session when necessary, and always after each period of sessions: i.e. the end of each term.

- Ongoing consultation takes place on an individual basis about individual learning needs and the group's consensus is always sought before any new direction or element is introduced.

- The social element is a very high priority throughout the programme.

- Learning about process, meeting artists and using their own lived experiences as a resource is a key element of the programme.

- Older people's contact and involvement with contemporary art and artists is essential to the exploration of new forms of expression and personal creativity. It contributes to the ongoing process of dealing with personal and social change in society.

- Enabling this kind of access to long term educational programmes, that are learner-centred and which work with learners on an equal footing has been essential in developing the museum's access beyond merely opening doors.

- Expanding the Museum's policy on exhibitions to incorporate artwork and work with special interest groups like older learners has also been crucial to this process.

OLDER LEARNERS AT THE BRITISH MUSEUM

The University of the Third Age (U3A) is a worldwide network of special interests groups which encourage people in their later years to take part in education for its own sake. No qualifications are required to join and no qualifications are awarded. It originated in France in 1972, where it was closely linked to universities, but when it arrived in Britain it became more of a self-help organisation, with most of the teaching supplied voluntarily by its students based on the commitment to co-operative learning. It remains a voluntary organisation – running an impressive and diverse range of activities including language classes, arts and crafts groups, music appreciation, creative writing, philosophy and bird watching. It has some 153,000 members in the UK, organised across the country and run by the participants themselves.

In 2003 the first British Museum / U3A Shared Learning project took place. Fifteen older learners, aged from 50 to 88 years, joined up to work with the Lifelong Learning team on a research project which lasted for ten weekly sessions. Each member of the group researched their own chosen object, using the Museum and the rest of the group as their resource. Their research resulted in a presentation to the rest of the group in the galleries and education centre. The presentations were moving, funny, impressive and quite unique. The museum benefited greatly from the project in that museum staff learned a lot about how older adults learn from objects, an area of research in museum education which is not yet highly developed.

The Shared Learning Project is now an annual event, with a different group taking part each time. The commitment to shared learning continues and is reflected in activities that benefit both the learners and the museum; for example, the production of a trail and exhibition, as well as the evaluation of displays in the galleries and of the British Museum's methods of interpretation.

Shared Learning Projects, involving the U3A's network, now happen all over the United Kingdom, including the National Maritime Museum, The Royal Opera House and a regional project concerned with entertainment in Sussex.

WORKING WITH OLDER LEARNERS IN MUSEUMS

- Give plenty of time to the process: Older people tend to move more slowly, spend more time in conversation and enjoy the social aspects of these interactions enormously. Be aware of respecting the dignity of older people and prepare new visitors for their first visit suggesting that they might want to 'dress-up' for the occasion, as older people are more often more formal in relation to visiting public buildings, especially if it is the first visit. Suggest that overcoats are left on the bus if they are being dropped off and collected at the entrance as this will avoid having to make a separate trip to the cloakroom.

- Be aware of the process of ageing: The physical aspects of ageing means that many older adults will need more time to move from one place in the gallery to another, and that adequate, comfortable seating in galleries should be provided. If groups need to be split up to use the lift and/or stairs to access another floor, arrange for a meeting point to reunite the group. They may need studio tools and furniture adapted to make it more comfortable and appropriate. Sight and hearing difficulties accelerate with age. Be sure to speak clearly and have magnifying glasses available.

- Photography or video: is recommended as an aide memoire and a visual document, as older people may have difficulty in recalling the visit and linking one event with the next.

- The language and point size used in labels, text panels and gallery guides should take into account the learners' prior knowledge and need for visual clarity. If hand-outs are being provided avoid passing them out in advance of the gallery visit, if individuals are using walking frames as they will need to keep both hands free.

- Lighting and floor surfaces should take into account those with physical difficulties – this is also good practice in working with any audience as there may be people with disabilities in any group.

- Orientation at the beginning of a visit is essential and all housekeeping arrangements should be covered before the content of the visit is outlined; be alert throughout the visit of potential difficulties that may arise with physical access.

4.4 Corporate groups

WHAT IS MEANT BY "CORPORATE GROUPS"?

Corporate groups can be defined as "adult groups linked with business life or the private sector". The relation of these groups to a museum or gallery can be of two different kinds:

- They can belong to companies that are the sponsors or business partners of the museum/gallery.

- They can be independent adult groups from a company that has no official relation to the organisation, but simply want to spend some time in the museum, doing some kind of cultural activity.

The most obvious difference between the two types of group is the economic relationship with the museum: in the case of corporate sponsors or business partners there may be a contractual arrangement requiring the museum to offer some sort of enrichment programme – guided tours, family days, behind the scenes tours, private views – to the employees.

The focus in this section is on the independent corporate groups who do not have a financial or contractual arrangement to be 'provided' with an education activity. Most of the advice, however, can be applied to sponsor groups as well.

Corporate groups, although being a very special audience for museums, are nevertheless an adult audience in their own right, with particular learning requirements and needs. Such groups are not made up exclusively of managers or directors, but can include staff at all levels in the company: people who might not visit the museum if not within the context of a collective activity with colleagues. In this sense, they can also be regarded as new audiences and as adult learners.

WHAT IS DISTINCTIVE ABOUT CORPORATE AUDIENCES?

The Kiasma Museum of Contemporary Art in Helsinki has recently been active in developing activities addressed to the business sector. It has also carried out a small piece of research in some European museums, to see how others were working with corporate groups as an adult, learning audience.

The results of their enquiries and the direct experience at Kiasma provide the following information:

- In developing programmes for corporate groups, museums have moved from a reactive to a proactive attitude. From simply responding to requests coming from the private sector, and adjusting existing activities or workshops to the needs of this new audience, museums are now designing, packaging and actively marketing new sets of learning activities and products to the corporate sector.

- Business groups, when visiting a museum on an organised occasion, expect to have a good and relaxing time with colleagues, rather than an 'educational experience'. This doesn't mean, however, that what they regard as a social event cannot have an educational impact, although in an enjoyable and entertaining way. It is just a matter of shaping the event in a way which takes into account the group's specific agenda.

- Being perceived mostly as a social event, the corporate group's visit to the museum usually requires a separate space and the provision of food and

From the catalogue of the exhibition Gli occhi del pubblico (Bologna, IBC-CLUEB, 2006)
Photo: Tano d'Amico

drink. It is popular for corporate groups to organise their own staff meetings or training days in a museum environment and connect it with a visit to the exhibition. This calls for specific meeting rooms and conference equipment, especially audio-visual facilities. As concerts or other performances are also sometimes part of the package, there can be the need for more hosting and staff presence. It is often more convenient to plan such visits after the museum's opening hours.

AN EXAMPLE FROM KIASMA CONTEMPORARY ART MUSEUM, HELSINKI

It had become evident that the regular one-hour guided tours or two to three-hour workshop sessions were not meeting the need of the corporate groups that visited Kiasma, and wanted to have a break in their working day or engage with art during their visit. A new form of service was developed for them: an activity tour which combines elements from guided tours and hands-on activities. The tour is flexible and can be used in varying situations and time schedules. The mediator uses a specially designed box, which includes the necessary

material for the visit. It can be used in the meeting room or in the gallery, and its main purpose is to trigger observation and discussion. The sessions are built around themes which start with the basic questions about contemporary art, for example the everyday materials used in art or contemporary forms of portrait and landscape.

4.5 Intercultural Learning

HERITAGE, CULTURE AND IDENTITY

Heritage, it is said, plays a role in making people feel at home, giving them a sense of place, and of belonging to a place. Cultural heritage contains both the material and immaterial remains of history. Monuments, music, artefacts, architecture, archives, landscapes, dance steps, oral histories, photos and recipes are all part of it. Taken together they are part of the 'cultural luggage' that migrants carry with them, to be both challenged and changed by what they find in the new countries in which they settle.

What counts as culture is the consequence of a dynamic process. It gives meaning and value to things and ideas. People who have conditions, circumstances and experiences in common create a group culture. At the same time, every individual belongs to several groups. Sometimes a person makes a choice to belong to a certain group, for instance a professional group. One is born into other groups, for example, family, nation, gender, or ethnicity. These aspects – skin colour, race, sex, for example – are fixed. But they are imbued with different meanings in different contexts and shaped according to ideas and values, custom and everyday practice. Individuals might be *born* female, for example, but they *learn* their gender role from within their community. In different communities or eras, learned roles can take very different cultural forms or meanings.

Over time all cultures change and develop through contact with other cultures. The characteristics of national cultures, together with national languages and histories are formed in the crucible of international exchange, trade, war and migration. Some cultures are more powerful than others in this process of exchange and are able to exert greater influence. But history teaches that national fortunes can wax and wane. American culture was not always the most powerful in global terms. The rapid economic transformation of China, and to some extent India, for example, is already beginning to challenge the current pattern of western cultural domination.

Intercultural contacts between people with different cultural backgrounds present experiences that are both common and unique. Common experiences that involve finding shelter, working, social exchange, love and relationships, travelling, making music - all play a role in the life of people anywhere in the world. But the way they are conducted and experienced is everywhere shaped and given meaning by social and cultural difference.

INTERCULTURAL LEARNING

Intercultural learning is a term used in various European countries, including the Netherlands, to describe work with participants from minority racial, ethnic and cultural backgrounds, whose experiences may include racial discrimination or racial prejudice. It is sometimes referred to as multi-cultural learning or diversity.

However, just as people from the same ethnic group can belong to different cultural groups or sub-groups, one could say that every open exchange of knowledge and life experience between two or more people is intercultural learning.

Intercultural issues, immigration and language learning, intolerance, racism and discrimination, are challenges faced by all European countries to a greater or lesser extent. As part of a dynamic and complex society, museums cannot ignore their role in all of these issues, and especially in the work they do with adult audiences.

INTERCULTURAL PROGRAMMES

A good example of intercultural learning is to be found in the Intercultural (Museum) Programmes (IP), funded by the Dutch Ministry of Education, Culture and Science in cooperation with the Netherlands Museums Association between 1998 and 2004. Intercultural learning according to IP is based on acknowledging and respecting the

differences and similarities between people and groups.

The aim of the project was to recognise and acknowledge cultural diversity in the heritage sector, while diversifying both public, staff and programming of museums and other heritage institutions. Subjects such as "Diversity marketing" or "How to diversify the museum staff" were brought to the attention of professionals in the field. In museum programming this concerns education, presentation and collections. Presentations and collections on the history of migrants, colonialism, slavery and Islamic heritage were promoted. An important pilot project on adult learning concerned the publication called 'History of our own surroundings. Museum and Heritage project for Dutch as a second language'

The project preceded the point at which a (paid) citizenship course became compulsory for migrants in the Netherlands after the events of 9/11 in 2001. Government thinking at that time, as in many other European countries, was tending to equate cultural integration with assimilation,

and to place most of the responsibility on migrants to adapt to the mores and values of the settled majority.

The project helped to promote the use of heritage places – museums, archives, archaeological sites and monuments – in order to learn more about the language and history of the Netherlands. The project was developed through the close cooperation between museum and heritage education workers with language teachers and learners.

Special learning packages were produced, each of which consisted of three lessons: the first and last to take place in the language school, the second to inform a site visit to a museum, archive or heritage site. All the packages were published, with separate material for teachers and learners. For those who wanted to make their own packages, a short manual was prepared to help them do so.

LANGUAGE LEARNING IN THE MUSEUM

Museums can provide a rich resource for learning a second language or developing skills in a first. Objects,

Assyriomania

Photo: British Museum, London

artworks and displays can trigger immediate responses, memories or cultural reference points to be discussed or shared with another learner, as illustrated by these two brief case studies. Museum educators wishing to develop this type of work should contact local teachers of adult language skills.

Peer to peer learning

A special simple but very effective programme was experimented in the Netherlands House of Parliaments exhibition called Aletta Jacobs and the longing for politics. Aletta Jacobs (1853-1929) was the first female medical doctor with a university degree and a famous suffrage fighter. It was a unique experience, but one that can be adapted by other museums. Two groups of learners were involved: a Dutch women's self-guided learning group that had existed for twenty years and a group of adult immigrant learners of the Dutch language that were trained by a teacher in formal adult education. Both groups arrived at the same moment. The only instruction they received was: go with one person from the other group through the exhibit and talk about anything you see and find interesting using the five

'w's of journalism – who, what, where, when, why). The participants were encouraged to ask questions such as: Why is this photo there? Do you know what this object is?

Both groups were very enthusiastic about the intercultural encounter that the visit of the exhibit had brought them. The teachers noticed individuals speak who normally would have been quiet in the class. A language learner wrote:
I really like the exhibit. It is interesting because for the first time I hear and see something about old habits in the Netherlands. I like the contact with the Dutch ladies, very interesting because I learned new words and another way of speaking.

A first-language Dutch speaker of the women's group said:
It was nice to go with someone. He was really surprised because I told him that in my youth we couldn't wear trousers as women and that married women were under the jurisdiction of their husbands, so that until the law changed in 1956 our signature was invalid after marriage. He was very shocked by the fact that we weren't allowed to live together outside of marriage.

Other comments included:
The form of going together with learners of Dutch as a second language was very special. I look at them as if they don't know so much, but she had done a higher secondary school than me. She could read very well, just not speak.

I have realised how difficult the Dutch language is through her.

This experience clearly shows that integration is and should be a two-sided process.

English for Speakers of Other Languages (ESOL) at the British Museum

English for Speakers of Other Languages (ESOL) is part of a British government strategy for supporting adults with literacy, language and numeracy difficulties and for whom English is not their mother tongue. Of the estimated seven million adults in the UK who have difficulty with basic skills, about one million of them have a first language other than English. The learners come from settled ethnic communities; some are refugees and asylum seekers; increasingly they are migrant workers from

Europe, with widely different educational backgrounds.

ESOL is an important part of the British Museum's social inclusion and audience development work. Museum collections are used to promote the skills of listening, speaking, reading and writing English. Learners study world cultures, often their own, and are able to learn through objects in a dedicated and stimulating environment.

The Museum organises approximately 45 tours a year for ESOL learners, using the main collections and sometimes special exhibitions. Each session lasts 90 minutes, starting in the Education Centre and then introducing learners to the Enlightenment, Egyptian and Assyrian Galleries. The session concludes in the African galleries with an emphasis on contemporary art and further independent learning for those who are interested to continue. ESOL college tutors are also made welcome and encouraged to make use of the museum with their students.

GOOD PRACTICE FOR MUSEUMS BASED ON THE NETHERLANDS EXPERIENCE

Identity

See learners as complex individuals with significant personal histories in their own right. Avoid focusing on only one aspect of their identity. Remember that identity is multiple and dynamic. The borders between cultures are variable. Be sure that the use of words like 'we' and 'them', 'our ancestors', 'others', 'strangers' do not exclude your learners. Present yourself as someone who also has a history – with your own share of contradictions and conflicts. Space for your life history gives space and trust for learners to tell about their life histories.

Content

Use heritage to illustrate and explore intercultural exchange. Music - such as jazz - is a result of the mixing of diverse musical traditions. Some inventions or discoveries that seem new in some parts of the world, were already known in other parts. The Chinese and Koreans knew the art of printing books, for example, before Gutenberg 'discovered' how to do it. New York already had a name before it was called New Amsterdam.

Science, algebra and mathematics are inconceivable without the Islamic-Arab world. For European countries with colonial pasts, the shared heritage of slavery and trade, for example, have very different meanings, depending on which side of the exchange your ancestors experienced.

Encounter

Use heritage as a source of intercultural exchange. Any artefact, building, or site can lead to the exploration of universal themes like housing, work, safety, care, play etc. Traces from the past carry multiple meanings. Show your interest in learners' perspective and ideas. Respect their opinions. Try to ask open questions. What do you keep, collect or take with you? What do you think this object is? Why do you think this happened? Open questions lead to talking. Try to avoid learners feeling attacked by questions that carry a negative judgment. Create and share knowledge in empowering ways rather than didactic ways.

Surprise

Make space for learners to develop their own interests and to exercise initiative. On visits to cultural sites give learners space and time to explore on their own and plenty of time to think about any questions they might have.

Emotion

Make sure there is a direct connection between what they are looking at or handling, and the original. Let them touch the archive paper, go to the actual site of the monument, make an interview with eye-witnesses.

Diversity

Look for diversity in the photos, film and source materials you are using. Check which images you use. Many will be racist, some will be culturally inappropriate. In time these can become a source of critical examination but not at the first or second meeting. Negotiate and cooperate with migrant and minority learners, through their organisations, on an equal basis. Build strong partnerships with their representatives.

Remember that collections are merely selections of the period in which they were collected, based on the ideas and concerns of the collectors. What is seen as important enough to keep in a collection reveals as much about the authority, influence and power of the collectors as about the merits of the selected objects.

Imagery

Double check any images. Who is speaking? Who is acting? Who takes initiatives? It is quite likely that the historical source will reveal prejudice, racism or anti-semitism. Take time to explore and discuss how this works. Emphasise the contextual, historical and changeable nature of all ideas. Encourage learners to recognise stereotyped ideas and to be critical about them. Try to counteract unsubstantiated personal opinion.

Pedagogy

Present learners with clear aims and objectives for the programme. Negotiate what they might want to learn and be clear about what you expect of them. Challenge them to make choices. Try to be concrete. Use different approaches. Recognise the significance of different learning styles. Involve artists, musicians and drama specialists to vary the approach. Encourage experiential and active learning rather than formal instruction. Make use of all five senses.

Language

Pay extra attention to your use of language. Don't use superfluous jargon. When you ask a question, encourage learners to answer first in their mother tongue and then work together to construct responses in the new language they are learning. Encourage them to keep a record of the new words they are learning.

Legacy

Leave a legacy from the visit in the museum, archive, monument or website. For instance, write a letter to the archive about the visit, make a photographic record, or write in the museum's visitor book. With the prior permission of learners, invite the press or radio to join you at the monument. Working towards leaving a legacy is rewarding for both learners and teachers.

4.6 Inclusive learning

Inclusive learning is a term used by some museums to reflect their commitment to non-traditional approaches with a wide cross section of audiences and learners. It is intended as a counter to those institutional and educational practices that serve to reinforce exclusion.

UNDERSTANDING SOCIAL EXCLUSION

Social exclusion takes many forms. It can be direct or indirect and can involve whole groups as well as specific individuals. It is rooted in the economic inequalities of social class, race and gender. But it also has physical dimensions – to do with disability and physical impairment, as well as geographical dimensions – to do with territory, distance and isolation.

The main challenges facing museums with regard to social exclusion are:

Identifying and removing common institutional barriers – such as entrance fees that disadvantage those on low incomes, restricted opening hours, inappropriate staff attitudes and behaviour, inappropriate rules and regulations, exhibitions that do not reflect the diversity of communities or different learning styles, poor signage so that people cannot easily find their way around, absence of a sense of ownership and involvement by ordinary people, absence of adequate facilities for people with disabilities and physical impairments.

Sustainability and long-term resource issues. Short term projects may provide some quick gains, but a more significant contribution lies in the development of a long-term social inclusion strategy to extend cultural rights to currently excluded groups and communities.

The need for cultural change within museums as institutions. Putting social inclusion and equal opportunities at the heart of museum learning, rather than the periphery, means forming alliances with the representatives of excluded groups and challenging some of the more traditional values and practices of museums. Cultural change can be fostered through a combination of staff training, staff development and staff support to raise awareness and improve staff performance in relation to socially excluded communities and visitors.

Community ownership and community partnership. If social inclusion policies are to be fully effective, it is vital that individuals and representatives of excluded groups are involved in developing, implementing and evaluating the services provided. Establishing and maintaining these links is time-consuming but every effort should be made to build upon community consultation and partnership.

Responding to the ever-changing ICT environment. The arrival of the 'information age' means that museums have an important role to play in developing a socially inclusive information strategy. Museums can be an important conduit for the creation of knowledge and sharing of information at local level, as well as enabling users to be in direct communication with museums across the wider world via the internet.

Integrating the work of museums with those of other services. The social inclusion activities of museums should not be seen in isolation. They will be most effective when they are integrated with the work of other agencies and organisations committed to reducing social exclusion.

Demonstrating benefits and outcomes. Museums can demonstrate their commitment to widening participation and strengthening social inclusion by;

- **Setting targets for widening participation**
- **Identifying social inclusion objectives**
- **Creating performance indicators**
- **Evaluating, reviewing and monitoring success**

From a theoretical viewpoint, it has been influenced by the thinking of Paulo Freire, whose ideas were outlined in section 2.

UNSPOKEN TRUTHS

A good example of Freire's influence on contemporary museum education is the 'Unspoken Truths' project. The project was a collaboration between the artist Ailbhe Murphy, two women's community development projects, and the Irish Museum of Modern Art in Dublin. Working class women were encouraged to explore aspects of their lives and their experiences of living in inner city Dublin and those of contemporary artists as evident in artwork that they experienced in IMMA's galleries. The dialogue between the artist and the women involved exploring their individual lives and discussing how artists, writers and poets also work through a similar process to create cultural artefacts. Drawing on radical theories in Community Development and Arts Education, Unspoken Truths also challenged the Museum's policy on access and engagement.

Taking as its starting point the authority of working class women's lived experience, the project came to life because of their commitment, willingness and determination to continue. An exhibition emerging from the project was displayed in four different venues across Ireland. The women involved made presentations at international conferences and a book and video documenting the project were both published.

When the project ended, the women continued to be involved in projects and programmes organised by the Irish Museum of Modern Art and through their own networks in Community Development. The artist, Ailbhe Murphy, continued to work with other groups in collaborative projects. And the museum now runs a programme entitled 'Focus on' ... for community groups which is based on the model created by Unspoken Truths involving, on average, 20 different groups each year.

EXCLUDED AUDIENCES: OFFENDERS OR PRISONERS
Rebibbia Nuovo Complesso

In 2004 the social co-operative Cecilia and Eccom (European Centre for Cultural Organisation and Management) developed a training course, financed by the Province of Rome, for assistants in archaeological excavations. The course was for ten offenders, aged 40 to 61 years old, who were inmates of Rebibbia Nuovo Complesso, the biggest prison in Rome. The training course lasted eleven months and provided 500 hours of training, through three modules: the History of the Ancient World; Methodologies and Techniques of Archaeological Excavations; and Care of the Green Areas within Archaeological Sites. At the end of the course, participants took an exam and afterwards received a Diploma. In addition Cecilia and Eccom wanted to assess the possibility of creating a labour co-operative, to include offenders, which could possibly manage an archaeological area which had been discovered within the prison grounds.

The prison is situated along the Roman road, Via Tiburtina and the whole area is extremely rich in archaeological sites related to the Roman period. Two years earlier, archaeologists had discovered within Rebibbia a Roman cemetery and a water cistern, both dating from the I-III centuries A.D. In the cemetery there were 85 tombs containing human skeletons - mainly of young men - and poor objects buried with the dead, such as lamps, ceramics, glass bowls and vases. As part of their course the offenders were able to clean and mark these ancient objects.

The experience of the training stimulated considerable enthusiasm and knowledge among the participants as well as doing wonders for their sense of self esteem and achievement. One of the men decided to continue his formal education in the field of cultural heritage at University; another one – who is a sailor and a diver of great experience - is going to work as a guide for archaeological diving tours all along the Mediterranean coasts.

The *Antiquarium*
A natural evolution of the training course, and of the practical activities undertaken on the site, was suggested by the participants themselves, who wanted to share their knowledge with other offenders and all the people who – for one reason or another – came into the prison. They wanted to tell the story of the objects and of the earliest origins of Rebibbia.

The idea became reality when the group started working at the development of a permanent exhibition of archaeological artefacts within the prison. The display of objects is accompanied by a storytelling process, in which the storytellers - supported by archaeologists, restorers and architects - are the offenders themselves, and the story told is about the history of a living part of Rome.

The offenders have learned technical skills and abilities related to archaeological and museological work, as well as being active in the storytelling process, enabling them to communicate to other people what they have learnt and discovered. In the process of discovering the past, they unearthed fascinating links between the past and present – to do with slavery and migration, poverty and incarceration - which has led to have a deeper consciousness of common roots and shared identity, as well as a better understanding of historical and personal development.

ADULTS WITH LEARNING DISABILITIES:
The Amazing Rembrandts Exhibition at The Amstelkring Museum, Our Lord in the Attic, Amsterdam
A group of adults with learning disabilities visited the Rijksmuseum where they came face to face with Rembrandt's wonderful paintings. The encounter made a great impression. Later, back in the studio, out came the books of Rembrandt reproductions. Pens and brushes were taken up: the results were astounding. The remarkable artists transformed Rembrandt's masterpieces into colourful paintings with a wholly

'Girl in a Window'
Artist: Piet Schopping

The painting has been made after seeing an exhibition at the Rijksmuseum, and is inspired by Rembrandt. With his own fiery style the artist puts faces, copied from a magazine or book, onto paper or canvas. He hardly talks, yet has a huge fascination for language, storing fragments of text that he comes across in daily life in his head, later reworking them in paintings and drawings which are powerful and direct.

personal slant. Forty-five works were selected for The Amazing Rembrandts, an exhibition at Amsterdam's Amstelkring Museum, also known as Our Lord in the Attic, a house from Rembrandt's own time containing a 'secret' church. The paintings are poignant, touching, intense and surprising.

This project differs from some adult learning projects in that the participants, adults with learning disabilities, were all experienced artists in their own right. They had been trained as artists for many years and had had exhibitions before. This however was their first exhibition in a museum, where both critics and the public considered them as 'real' artists. Therefore the 'inclusion' in this case, was the recognition and inclusion of a group of artists in a museum who had not before been regarded as artists. Another form of inclusion which occurred as a result of this project was the inclusion of the visitors who, through this kind of art, became acquainted with a new form of art they weren't familiar with.

There are several ways to consider the project as an adult learning project:

- The participants, in this case adults with learning disabilities, were so inspired by their visit and guided tour in the Rijksmuseum that they afterwards expressed themselves in their own 'language' – art – in such a way that it had museum-quality.

- The artists forged a strong link with the museum, talked to journalists and gave them guided tours. This enriched the experience beyond the initial visit and artistic response.

- By showing, celebrating, and validating the work, the museum brought a totally different audience to the museum, people that never had been to any museum, let alone to an art exhibition. Many of them worked in institutions for people with disabilities, or had learning-disabled family members or had a learning disability themselves. The new audience became acquainted with Rembrandt's work and with the Amstelkring Museum, both through the 'Amazing Rembrandts' exhibition and in the way the exhibition was set up.

4.7 Case study: adult learning at the British Museum

The British Museum was one of the first UK museums to appoint a Head of Lifelong Learning. The remit was not only to continue the strong tradition of adult education at the museum, but also, as the new title implied, to develop new audiences and new ways of promoting adult learning.

The existing education programme of lectures, study days, gallery talks, etc., was rethought in order to position the Museum as a centre of cultural debate connecting contemporary issues to the historical collections. For example:

- The season of events supporting Forgotten Empire, a major exhibition on Ancient Persia, included a debate in partnership with the Guardian newspaper entitled 'The unbroken arc: what ancient Persia tells us about modern Iran'.

- A strong programme of cultural events including film, literature, music and poetry makes connections between the collections and the contemporary arts and aims to appeal to a new generation of Londoners who have not traditionally thought of the British Museum as a place to go.

- The course programme for adults was also redeveloped. In partnership with Birkbeck University of London a unique set of courses was devised, World Arts and Artefacts, which reflect the global nature of the museum's collections, a recognition of different learning styles and a commitment to learning from objects. Part-time adult students can sign up for one off practical courses such as Indian textiles or Arabic calligraphy. These can be combined with historical and contextual studies of aspects of world arts to build up a portfolio of qualifications leading to a degree.

ADULT LEARNERS' WEEK

Adult Learners Weeks take place in several European countries and can function as good catalysts to design and stage new and innovative museum activities addressed to adults during the designated period.

In the UK, Adult Learners' Week is an annual, national festival of adult learning, organised by NIACE (the national organisation for adult learning in England and Wales). It involves hundreds of thousands of learners taking part in different learning activities across the country, as well as events, publications, media coverage, conferences and award ceremonies.

The British Museum's participation in Adult Learners' Week typically starts with an Open University Day at the Museum, inviting people to sign up for part-time programmes, through a varied programme of talks and activities which link Open University courses with specific museum collections. Special family learning activities are also scheduled to take place during Adult Learners' Week, to reflect the significant role that adults play in their children's learning when they visit the museum in family groups. This has included the opportunity to take part in drawing activities, try calligraphy and to watch artists demonstrate their work in the public courtyard of the Museum.

VOLUNTEERS FACILITATING LEARNING: 'HANDS ON' AT THE BRITISH MUSEUM

Every day, in very many of the galleries of the British Museum, eight or so small objects are placed on a handling table in the care of a 'Hands On' volunteer. The purpose is to enable visitors to have a direct and personal experience of the museum through touching and talking about the objects. Touching objects reveals something extra about their qualities which is not evident when they are behind glass - a Palaeolithic hand axe always prompts a strong reaction, for example

The thumb fits there, your fingers go here and this fits in your palm. It's so personalised, you held it in your hand and you used it … I've got small hands and it fits just there. You imagine you're in touch with the person that made it.

The programme is designed for visitors of all ages, not just children. Object handling is regarded as a tool of critical analysis as well as a sensual and emotional experience.

Holding things used to be for kids, places like this when I was young, guards tutting at you if you ever went near anything. It's the first time you can see, feel and touch and it really brings it home especially when the person says this is 350,000 years old, it brings it alive.

The role of the Hands On volunteer is crucial. As with guiding in the galleries, it is a medium of interpretation which offers social contact, but is more interactive and flexible as the volunteers work with the experiences and reactions of the visitor. The museum sees the training of volunteers (over 300 in total across many aspects of the museum's work) as part of its adult learning mission. The Hands On training for example is a big commitment from both museum staff and new recruits. It consist of five one day modules, run by the Learning Department and with the participation of curators and visitor services staff.

The Autobiographical Approach Cradle to Grave:
What's Your Story?

The Gallery of Living and Dying at the British Museum, sponsored by the Wellcome Trust, shows how different cultures, in different historical periods and contexts, have contributed to their own health and wellbeing. Objects on display include a giant Easter Island statue from 1000 AD and a modern sculptural interpretation of the Mexican Day of the Dead.

Down the middle of the gallery is an installation – Cradle to Grave – illustrates the medical journey of one western man and woman, who are reckoned to consume about 14,000 pills in the average course of their lifetime. The timelines of the man and woman are illustrated with personal memorabilia, photographs and documents, documenting key moments in their lives. The installation was created by a doctor, a textile artist and a video artist and attracts considerable attention and discussion.

The museum recently invited the two artists to run a workshop called What's Your Story? Participants worked with the artists to develop their own versions of the journey, inspired by the installation. Those who signed up for the workshop were asked to bring the contents of their medicine cabinet, a selection from their photograph album showing significant life events, and any objects which they thought related to their own health and wellbeing. With the use of video and photography, their creations became part of the museum display.

The small group taking part were recruited through open invitation in the gallery and targeted publicity to health centres, nursing schools and medical museums. The ideas underpinning the project along with the artists, the access manager and a curator have developed into an outreach arts project with a group of inmates in Pentonville Prison.

The project was just one example of the many through which the museum's collections are related to the broad threads of human experience – health, religion, ageing – and the aspirations of adult learners to interpret and re-interpret their culture and their lives.

It is also exemplary of a now not infrequent autobiographical approach adopted with adults, consisting in using museum objects to trigger reminiscence and encourage the re-visiting of one own's personal story.

African Gallery dancing

Photo: Benedict Johnson, British Museum, London

Section 5

5.1 Why is environment important?

Adult learning in a museum can be the result of participation in structured educational activities or projects. It can also happen informally during a museum visit, as a result of free interaction between individual visitors, objects, artworks or artefacts, and the museum space itself. Adults learn much on their own and this means that museums, as places of informal and individual learning, should strive to offer their visitors the best possible conditions to support this learning process. The museum environment plays an important role in promoting understanding of the works, effectiveness in raising the intellectual curiosity of the users and involving them in a unique experience, rich in cultural and emotional values. Visitors who feel physically comfortable, welcomed and orientated in museum spaces will enjoy their visit more and learn more as a result.

The relevance of this subject led the European Museum Forum to devote its 2005 Workshop to this theme, the conclusions of which can be read on:

www.collectandshare.eu.com under "reports".

The importance of the environment to learning is also recognised in the UK Museums Libraries and Archive Council's best practice framework for access and education, "Inspiring Learning for All", where it refers to 'Places - Creating an inspiring and learning environment that supports learning.'

5.2 Some elements to be considered

The environment in European museums has evolved quite significantly in the last three decades, due to a number of factors including:

- The adoption of new materials and new technical devices which have proved essential in improving exhibition design (for example, polycarbonates instead of glass; plastic materials instead of wood).

- Improved conservation techniques which have a direct impact on exhibition design.

- The use of multimedia and new technologies.

- The recognition of the importance of teamwork in exhibition development.

- Changing public and institutional views and expectations of what a museum should provide for its visitors.

Based on research conducted by the European Museum Forum, which, since 1977 has inspected more than 1600 museums to assess innovation for its European Museum of the Year Award, here are some elements which illustrate the evolution of the museum environment in recent years, with a specific focus on exhibition and display techniques. These are not meant to be definitive because all museums are different. However, they should provide food for thought and discussion when considering the museum environment and its impact on learning.

Wharf

Photo: The German Emigration Centre, Bremerhaven

THE PHYSICAL COMFORT OF VISITORS

It is often said that museum visitors vote with their feet, quite literally. Visiting a museum may well be exciting and involving, but in physical terms, it is often tiring. Giving focussed attention to paintings or exhibits, together with a lot of listening, walking, moving around and standing, makes for a heady mix of concentrated intellectual and physical tension that is not part of most people's everyday behaviour. Despite all efforts to make an exhibition interesting, or to assemble the most important masterpieces together in one gallery, the average visitor feels exhausted by the experience within about two hours. A welcoming museum tries to minimise this effect by creating restful areas including benches, chairs, and other opportunities to take a breather, despite the familiar limitations of design restrictions, space, fire and safety regulations.

The National Museum of Iceland recently introduced two interesting innovations: a bench equipped with a telephone receiver for listening to a recorded text fixed at one of the two extremities so that visitors can easily turn 180° and focus on elements on display in different areas of the room.

In the same museum visitors can make use of a room equipped with a bed complete with pillow, sheets and blankets, to be used by museum-goers if they feel tired, although the museum is not very large.

VISITORS' ORIENTATION

Museum and gallery orientation and signage caters for a wide variety of age, social, national, cultural and other special interest groups, and relies on a mix of audio, visual and digital aids to capture their attention. In addition, increasing museum awareness about how to welcome different learners, each with his or her own combination of learning needs, interests and styles, requires different kinds of communication existing side by side. If the implications are well understood, and done well, the results are unobtrusive but helpful and effective. If they are done badly, the proliferation of numbers, colours, codes and keywords can make the use of competing narrative, symbols and audio information seem over-complicated and counter-productive.

Similarly, an over-directed route march through the museum can actually prevent visitors discovering the treasures along the journey in their own way and at their own pace.

THE CO-EXISTENCE OF OLD AND NEW

Trying to make a museum a welcoming, communicative and learning-friendly place sometimes remains as wishful thinking, because of the restrictions and limitations imposed by the building and also by the presence of old facilities and equipment which might be regarded as museum pieces themselves.

For example, old showcases which display materials in a strictly taxonomic order are seen as testimonies of the museological approach of the 18th-19th centuries.

Changing the museum environment for a temporary exhibition can be more successful, because it presents the opportunity to view the environment afresh and to design a space especially to complement the works.

Care needs to be taken when renovating parts of existing exhibits

Freud

Photo: Het Dolhuys Museum, Haarlem

through "add-ons" or the addition of new elements to existing ones. Due consideration must be given to the new environment which is being created.

This process can result in clashes between the old and the new, which may be aesthetically disturbing, or just simply misleading, because the old element neutralises the innovative drive of the new one. For example, why leave an old showcase crammed with objects and captions next to a well-designed computer unit with touch screen, digital images and sounds, which can much more effectively give information about the artefacts?

SCREENS

Visual communication has moved with the times. First cinema screens were installed in the larger museums, then televisions, videos and DVDs. The widespread use of computers, made resource-rich by increasingly sophisticated digital technology, is now an important information and education tool in the museum.

Screens connected to DVDs and computers provide considerable opportunities for communication, although their impact on visitors is not always predictable. Information screens, such as touch screens, whereby visitors can negotiate their way through icons to sources of information, or narrative screens, whereby different stories are relayed, provide both individual and group learning opportunities. They can be supplemented by video projectors that turn entire walls into large talking surfaces.

The Imperial War Museum in Manchester, for example, has used screens to great effect, projecting images into entire rooms in ways that immerse visitors in a drama of sight and sound through which they can walk. This is achieved using a simple slide projector rather than anything more sophisticated, illustrating the importance of selecting the right tool – old or new – for the job.

LIFE-SIZED MODELS

Life-sized models have a long history, especially in natural history museums. They went out of fashion for a while when more minimalist approaches to exhibition design became more common but they are currently experiencing a revival. Life-sized models attract visitors' curiosity and may provide a sense of authenticity to the museum experience, despite the competition from more technically sophisticated forms of virtual reality. Their strength lies in the fact that they are three dimensional, tangible and big. They can be used to introduce a human element into displays of habitat, machinery and transportation, or to demonstrate how objects were used and experienced in the past.

Models can be realistic, or evocative, or metaphysical - depending on the theme and purpose of the exhibition. Their use is a matter of taste, choice, resources, the technical ability of the designer and the philosophy of the museum. Realistic models are very expensive, but cheap versions produce a cheap effect and can damage the credibility of the museum or the display. Metaphysical models are often more effective than realistic ones if they are able to suggest a special artistic or poetic dimension to an exhibition. But if they are either cheap or too intellectual they do not work well.

Wax models at the exhibition "Bombings on Milan" organised by the Historic Collections of the City of Milan

Photo: Photographic Archive - Historic Collections of the City of Milan

INTRIGUING PRESENCES

Among the technological innovations introduced in the museum's space, a special role is played by devices that are hard to categorise but which include machines with human-like behaviour and which represent "intriguing presences" for visitors. These interventions may look like human beings or animals (animatronics), interacting with visitors in the most realistic way, and even engaging them in conversation if operated at distance by a skilled operator. They may retain the appearance of industrial artefacts, like the robots which welcome you at the Museum of Communication in Berlin playing football among themselves or with the visitors. These devices are successfully replacing "talking heads" which were always a difficult to use technology, popular in the early 1990s, and consisting of projecting an image of a real person (a protagonist of history, for example) onto a model face.

Avatars have a different role: they are conceived as substitutes for guides, accompanying visitors in the museum tour in different ways according to the technology adopted or the philosophy of the project. Virtual avatars are nowadays becoming more popular and seem to be the future of this application, particularly for integration with the Internet.

5.3 Creating a learning-friendly environment

Here are a few things to think about:

- Consult with audiences to create an environment that suits their needs. This may include opening times of the museum, entry areas, seating and other rest areas, signage, disability access, and the types of interpretation or learning resources provided. There are many ways to consult: by establishing a group of audience advisors, by interviewing or surveying existing audiences, by going outside of the museum to ask people who don't attend what would entice them to try it out, or by speaking with common-interest users, such as visitors with physical disabilities.

- Assess the museum entrance and entrance hall as if you were a first- time visitor. Are the spaces inviting, is the entrance clearly marked, can even the inexperienced visitor find his or her way easily, are there seats?

- Adding signposting and other information for different visitors groups can be confusing. Look at all the signs and symbols from a visitor's point of view. Are there too many or not enough? Are there other solutions?

- Use multimedia wisely and inventively: the most modern and sophisticated is not always the best or most effective. First ask yourself, what is the purpose? Then devise the best solutions for your resources.

- Life-sized models can be an asset for a presentation. But good models are expensive whereas cheap, badly made, models can spoil they effect. Models should be in keeping with the rest of the exhibition both in content and design.

- Pay attention to the physical comfort of your visitors: create enough rest areas, or provide free, portable seats for visitors to carry. Benches can also be combined with information: headsets, screens, written information. But be aware of what is adequate to promote learning and what is too much and overwhelming.

5.4 A case study

The importance of the environment is even more evident in those museums which are located in old buildings, palaces, historic houses, or which include monuments or sites of industrial heritage as part of their collections, such as in the following example. Guided tours, when designed in an innovative and involving way for the visitors, are one way to approach these very special artefacts.

Museu da Água, Lisbon

The mission of the Museu da Água is to encourage visitors to be more aware of protecting the environment and of the values inherent in Lisbon's historical, documental, monumental and cultural heritage. The museum invites a wide variety of visitors to explore these concerns through educational, animation and cultural activities.

The museum focuses on:

- Creating and supporting a dynamic programme, with initiatives that meet the interests of a wide variety of visitors and compete with the spread of other leisure activities.

- Attracting new audiences and educating wider, more demanding and better-informed visitors, by establishing with them a close and lasting relationship.

- Contributing to environmental education, through programmes aimed at both children and adults.

- Creating forums for reflection, dialogue and discussion of themes such as the environment, water, the historical heritage, the Baroque and related study fields.

- Adjusting the museum's role to the challenges posed by social change to become more actively engaged with the concerns of contemporary society.

Themed visits and cultural walks take place related to the Museum's permanent and, where possible, temporary exhibitions. These may also include other parts of the Museum, for example the Aqueduct. These themed visits for organised groups try to meet a diverse range of interests and needs. Visitors discuss and learn, according to the route and the theme chosen by the learners. Visits can take place in Portuguese or another language, and are held throughout the year. In many cases, development of the theme and visit involve another partner working closely with museum staff.

Themes

- **The Baroque: The Queen refreshes herself.** This walk focuses on an aspect of the social history of the Aqueduct and the spirit of the Baroque by recreating a journey undertaken by the Royal Family, the Court, and the common people through the Águas Livres Aqueduct as they travelled from Mafra to Queluz.

- **Geology: Geo-Aqueduct.** The springs of the Aqueduct and the Hydra-geology of the Carenque-Caneças region, are the subject of this visit. A geological approach to the Aqueduct, the Mãe de Água das Amoreiras and the Geology of Lisbon is pursued. These visits are organised in partnership with the Geology Department of the Faculdade de Ciências of the Universidade de Lisboa.

Cultural Walk – Geo Aqueduct

Photo: Museu da Água, Lisbon

- **Symbolism: The Paths of Water.** In collaboration with Quinta da Regaleira and Palácio de Queluz, the visitors are invited to experience the element water in its three dimensions: as an esoteric symbol, in Quinta da Regaleira, as "divertissement" in the gardens of Palácio de Queluz and, as a moral value at the springs of the Águas Livres Aqueduct.

- **Change through time: From the Patriarcal to the Chafariz do Vinho.** The Water Museum in collaboration with the Chafariz do Vinho has renewed the journey that takes visitors through the underground galleries from the Patriarcal (Principe Real) to the Chafariz do Vinho (Praça da Alegria). The Chafariz do Vinho has been refurbished and adapted to its new function as a wine tasting venue.

- **Ecology and Cultural Heritage: From the Aqueduct to the Palácio Marquuês de Fronteira.** Walking across the majestic Águas Livres Aqueduct, over the Alcântara Valley, visitors contemplate a panoramic view of Lisbon before entering the Monsanto Natural Park, one of Lisbon's last havens. Just before the journey comes to an end the visitors are invited to appreciate the Church of S. Domingos de Benfica and the Palácio Marquês de Fronteira.

- **Aesthetics: Paths of Light.** This visit explores the aesthetic qualities of the Águas Livres Aqueduct, focusing on contrasts: heat and cool, light and shade, water and air.

- **History: Lisbon, the Aqueduct and the Earthquake.** This visit recreates the route taken by Jácome Ratton, a French trader living in Portugal in 1755, through the streets of the city to the safety of Alto da Cotovia, today know as Garden of Principe Real. The route also includes a stop at the Águas Livres Aqueduct where he saw, "on his feet", the destruction of the city of Lisbon on 1 November 1755.

(Over page) From the catalogue of the exhibition Gli occhi del pubblico (Bologna, IBC-CLUEB, 2006)

Photo: Isabella Balena

Section 6

The changing social roles of museums, with their increased emphasis on visitor and learner-centred approaches, has tremendous training implications for museum professional staff. Public policies concerned with widening participation, combating social exclusion, improving intercultural understanding and promoting cultural rights means that museum professionals have to become as knowledgeable about the wider world and their potential audiences as they are about their objects and exhibitions. They need a heightened awareness of the social and political context in which these policies originate and have significance. They also need to understand the significance of relating exhibition content and interpretation to the existing knowledge and background of prospective audiences, and to realise that most audience members will not have a specialist or academic knowledge of the subject

Although experience and systems differ widely across Europe, there is a good deal of shared understanding and consensus about the four areas in which competence is required when it comes to project planning and educational work: preparation, design and planning, delivery, and evaluation.

Preparation

- Shaping ideas

- Analysing context – in relation to audience, subject matter and institution

- Doing background research – in relation to collections, audience and learning styles

- Networking and partnership development

- Planning exhibitions and events

- Identifying training needs

- Securing appropriate staff development opportunities.

Design and planning

- Organisational skills: designing appropriate events, project management, financial planning, identifying and contacting potential audiences, and scheduling.

- Educational skills: Developing learning aims and objectives, identifying learning approaches, creating learning activities and producing teaching and learning materials.

Delivery

- Staging and presenting events

- Conducting the related educational activities.

Evaluation

- Monitoring and reviewing activities and events, both during and at the end of their existence.

- Measuring learning outcomes against set targets

- Researching partner and user satisfaction.

More specifically, museum educators involved in the informal provision of lifelong learning in museums need to be able to do a variety of different tasks. They must be able to:

- Devise and plan innovative educational programmes and activities that recognise the diverse needs of new and different audiences

- Work in partnership with audience and learner groups and/or their representatives in the planning, delivery and evaluation of activities

- Identify current and potential audiences and learners in ways that show understanding of their diverse needs

- Provide opportunities for existing audiences or learners to explore ideas and develop understanding relevant to their own needs and interests

- Provide opportunities for new and different audiences to represent and develop their specific cultural concerns

- Commission and produce educational and resource materials to meet the needs of diverse audiences

- Create learning environments that are accessible and user-friendly

- Evaluate the impact of learning activities on audiences or learners

- Devise, develop and evaluate the education and learning strategy of their organisation

- Contribute to, and help to shape, the interpretative strategy of their organisation.

The emerging training needs for museum and gallery educators are:

- Having a working knowledge of adult education theories and approaches

- Gaining insight into the social and political factors which shape and constrain the experiences of learners

- Developing programmes which help to promote creative thinking skills

- Developing programmes for self-directed learning

- Communicating with adult audiences using innovative approaches and techniques

- Documenting projects and activities effectively, for networking and dissemination purposes and as part of reflective evaluation

- Evaluating the impact of learning on adults participating in museum activities

- Building networks with external partners, audiences, and peers, locally, regionally, nationally and internationally

- Managing change.

Consequently the training programmes devised for staff development purposes should equip museum educators to:

Focus on learners: Innovations concerned with outreach, access and activity should start and proceed in relation to the needs and to the material and cultural circumstances of learners, rather than the needs and requirements of institutions. Outreach, contact outside of the museum or gallery, needs to be taken seriously as the first and most important point of contact with non-traditional learners.

Focus on the activity: How does the knowledge of the art or collections connect to the lived experience of learners? Dialogue and interactive teaching methods – concerned with developing creativity, problem-solving, critical thinking and tolerant and reflective attitudes– are much more likely to enhance learning than didactic transmission. Information-giving should respond to participants with different amounts of prior knowledge. Some of the conventions and rituals of museum and gallery settings may need to be modified and diversified in order to welcome new participants.

Focus on partnership: Recognise that widening participation to include non-traditional audiences is common to the concerns of both learning and culture. Working in partnership with educational providers, as well as with the communities and associations that represent the interests of learners, is the best way to respond positively to learners' needs and interests. Working in partnership should include the development of shared staff training and the development of opportunities across institutional boundaries.

Focus on equal opportunities and empowerment: Equal opportunities and respect for diversity and difference should be at the centre of the museum's work. Regular consultation, dialogue and collaboration should take place with the representatives of excluded groups.

Focus on research and development: Training support for museum educators should aim to ensure that staff are as knowledgeable and rigorous about participants as they are about their exhibits and collections.

From the catalogue of the exhibition Gli occhi del pubblico (Bologna, IBC-CLUEB, 2006)

Photo: Tano d'Amico

Section 7

Bibliography and web sites

ADULT LEARNING INSPECTORATE (2003), *Annual Report of the Chief Inspector,* London.
– (2002), Committed to Excellence, London.

AMBROSE T., PAINE C. (2006), *Museum Basics,* Routledge, London and New York (2nd edition).

American Association of MuseUms (2002), *Excellence in Practice: Museum Education Standards and Principles,* Washington D.C.
– (2000 a), *Code of Ethics for Museums 2000,* Washington D.C.
– (2000 b), *Museum Assessment program (MAP). Public Dimension Assessment Self-Study Workbook,* Washington D.C.
– (1992), *Excellence and Equity: Education and the Public Dimension of Museums,* Washington D.C.

AMIETTA P. L. (ed.) (2000), *I luoghi dell'apprendimento,* FrancoAngeli, Milano.

ANDERSON D. (1999), *A Common Wealth: Museums in the Learning Age,* report written for the Department for Culture, Media and Sport (UK), Stationery Office, London.

ASSOCIAZIONE PER L'ECONOMIA DELLA CULTURA, *Economia della cultura,* no. 3/2001 (themed issue on "Culture and Multiethnic Society"), 4/2004 (themed issue on "Culture and Social cohesion", ed. by BODO S., DA MILANO C.), 2/2006 (themed issue on "Access", ed. by DA MILANO C., DE LUCA M.), il Mulino, Bologna.

BARR J. (2005), *Dumbing Down Intellectual Culture: Frank Furedi, lifelong learning and museums* (available to download from http://www. collectandshare.eu.com/reports/index.aspx).
– (2004), *Cultural entitlement and what galleries and museums can contribute to adult learning,* (available to download from http://www.collectandshare. eu.com/reports/index.aspx).

BARTON D., TUSTING K. (2006), *Models of Adult Learning: a literature review,* NIACE/ NRDC.

BELANGER P. (2001), «New Visions of Lifelong Learning and Museums», in THINESSE-DEMEL J. (ed.), *Education as a Tool for Museums,* Final Report on the Socrates Project MUSAEAM, Budapest.
– (1994), «Lifelong learning: the dialectics of Lifelong education», in *International review of education,* n. 40, pp. 353-381.

BENSON C. (1989), *Art and the Ordinary. The report of the Arts Community Education Committee to the Arts Council and the Gulbenkian Foundation,* Arts Community Education Committee, Dublin.

BODO S. (ed.) (2003), *Il museo relazionale. Riflessioni ed esperienze europee,* Edizioni Fondazione Giovanni Agnelli Torino.

BODO S., CANTÙ S., MASCHERONI S. (ed.) (2007), *Progettare insieme per un patrimonio interculturale,* Quaderni ISMU 1/2007, Fondazione ISMU, Milano.

BODO S., CIFARELLI M. R. (ed.) (2006), *Quando la cultura fa la differenza. Patrimonio, arti e media nella società multiculturale,* Meltemi, Roma.

BORUN M., CHAMBERS M., CLEGHORN A. (1996), «Families are learning in Science Museums», in *Curator,* 39 (2), pp. 123-38.

BRAMBILLA RANISE G. (ed.) (2006), *Per un diritto al patrimonio culturale, monograph in L'integrazione scolastica e sociale,* vol. 5, n. 5, November 2006, Edizioni Erickson, Gardolo (Trento).

BRANCHESI L. (ed.) (2006), *Il patrimonio culturale e la sua pedagogia per l'Europa,* Armando editore, Roma.

CAILLÉT E., LEHALLE E. (1995), *À l'approche du musée. La médiation culturelle,* Presse Universitaire, Lyon.

CALIDONI M., RONDA R. (ed.) (2004), *La pratica educativa nei musei. I – I musei si presentano. II – L'esperienza di formazione,* Biblioteca "A. E. Mortara", Casalmaggiore.

CAMERON D. (1972), «The Museum: A Temple of the Forum», in *Journal of World History* 14, no. 1.

CATON J. (2004), *Museums as Places for Lifelong Learning: glossary of terms on education and access in museums,* IBC, Bologna.

CHADWICK A. (1999), «Museums and adult education: partners or competitors?», in B. Martin (ed.), *Adult education and the museum,* Final Report on the Socrates Project TM-AE 1-995-DE-1 supported by the DG XXII of the European Commission, DVV, Bonn.

CHADWICK A., STANNET A. (2000), *Museums and Adults Learning. Perspectives from Europe,* NIACE, London.

CITTÀ DI TORINO - SETTORE EDUCAZIONE AL PATRIMONIO CULTURALE (2006), *Un patrimonio di tutti. Musei e inclusione sociale,* Quaderni dei Musei Civici, n. 11, Torino
(available to download from http://www.comune. torino.it/museiscuola/esperienze/pdf/Quaderno_ 11.pdf)

CITTÀ DI TORINO - SETTORE MUSEI (2002), *Un museo, tanti pubblici. Condizioni di accessibilità per i visitatori anziani. Risultati di un'indagine,* Quaderni dei Musei Civici, n. 8, Torino
(available to download from http://www.comune. torino.it/museiscuola/esperienze/pdf/Quaderno_ 08.pdf)

CITTÀ DI TORINO and ISTITUTO PER I BENI ARTISTICI, CULTURALI E NATURALI DELLA REGIONE EMILIA ROMAGNA (2006), *Museums Tell Many Stories. A training experience for intercultural communication,* Torino.

COLLECT & SHARE (2005), *Good Practice, Training Needs, and Action Points*
(available to download from www.collectandshare. eu.com).

CLIVE S. (2003), *'Getting it Together' Grants Programme,* engage, London.

COUGHLAIN S., DRURY M., ECO-CNCI working party (2004), *A Policy Framework for Education, Community and Outreach work in the ten National Cultural Institutions,* Council of National Cultural Institutions, Dublin.

COUNCIL OF EUROPE (1998), Committee of Ministers, *Recommendation No. R (98) 5.*

CRAKE P., JOHNSON M. (2000), *Education Futures: lifelong learning,* Design Council -RSA, London.

DA MILANO C., DE LUCA, M. (ed.) (2006), *Attraverso i confini: il patrimonio culturale come strumento di integrazione sociale,* ECCOM/Compagnia di San Paolo, Roma.
– (2004), «La didattica del museo e del territorio negli anni '90», in C. Bodo, C. Spada (ed.), *Rapporto sull'economia della cultura in Italia, 1990-2000,* Il Mulino, Bologna.

DAVORAN A., MARSHALL C., McEVOY J. (1999), *Come to the edge,* Irish Museum of Modern Art, Dublin.
– (1996), *A Sense of Place,* Irish Museum of Modern Art, Dublin.

DAVERN A., MC GONAGLE D., O'DONOGHUE H., LEWIS R. (1996), *Intersections: Testing a World View,* Irish Museum of Modern Art, Dublin.

DAVIS S. (1994), *'By Popular Demand'. A strategic analysis of the market potential for museums and galleries in the UK,* Museums and Galleries Commission, London.

DE CARLI C. (ed.) (2003), *Education through art. I musei di arte contemporanea e i servizi educativi tra storia e progetto,* Edizioni Gabriele Mazzotta, Milano.

Department for Culture, Media and Sports (2000), *Centres for Social Change,* London.
– (1999), *Museums for the Many,* London.

DEPARTMENT FOR EDUCATION AND SKILLS (2003), *Bigger Pictures, broader Horizons: widening Access to Adult Learning in the Arts and Cultural Sectors,* London.

DIERKING L. (1989), «What research says to museum educators about the family museum experience», in *Journal of Museum Education,* 14 (2), pp. 9-11.

DI MAURO A., GALLONI V., SANI M. (ed.) (2006), *I musei incontrano i mondi degli adulti. Metodi ed esperienze di lifelong learning,* conference proceedings ("Musei e Lifelong learning: esperienze educative rivolte agli adulti nei musei europei", Bologna, Sala Auditorium Regione Emilia-Romagna, October 17th-18th, 2005 ; "L'età matura del museo. Incontro con i mondi degli adulti , IX Giornata Regionale di studio sulla Didattica Museale, Rovigo, Accademia dei Concordi, November 7th, 2005) Regione Veneto - IBC Regione Emilia-Romagna, Treviso.

DODD J., SANDELL R. (1998), *Building Bridges. Guidance for museums and galleries on developing new audiences,* Museums & Galleries Commission, London.
– (ed.) (2001), *Including Museums. Perspectives on Museums, Galleries and Social Inclusion,* University of Leicester, Research Centre for Museums and Galleries, Leicester.

DONNA M. A., MASCHERONI S., SIMONE V. (ed.) (2004), *Didattica dei musei. La valutazione del progetto educativo,* FrancoAngeli, Milano.

DUKE C. (2004), *Learning Communities: signposts from international experience,* NIACE, Leicester.

DURBIN G. (1996), *Developing museum exhibitions for lifelong learning,* London
– (2002), «Interactive Learning in the British Galleries 1500-1900», in *Interactive Learning in Museums of Art and Design,* conference paper (available to download from www.vam.ac.uk).

DRURY M. (1993), «Martin Drury: Extract from presentation to the Unspoken Truths Conference», in *Unspoken Truths: A Cultural Analysis,* Irish Museum of Modern Art, Dublin.

EUROPEAN CONSULTATION PLATFORM (2001), *Focus on lifelong learning,* EAEA, Bruxelles.

EUROPEAN MUSEUM FORUM (2004, 2005), *Conclusions from the European Museum Forum workshop* (Reports from 2004 and 2005 are available to download from http://www.collectandshare.eu.com/reports/index.aspx).

FAGAN R., DOWNEY M., MURPHY A., O'DONOGHUE H. (1996), *Unspoken Truths,* Irish Museum of Modern Art, Dublin.

FALK J., DIERKING L. (2000), *Learning from Museums. Visitor Experiences and the Making of Meaning,* Altamira Press, Walnut Creek.
– (1992), *The Museum Experience,* Whalesback Books, Washington.

FIELD J. (2001), *Promoting European Dimensions in Lifelong Learning,* NIACE , Leicester.

FINCHAM G. (2005), *Lifelines 22. Inspiring Adults: literacy, language and numeracy in the museums, libraries and archives sector,* NIACE, Leicester.

FLEMING T., GALLAGHER A. (2000), *Even her nudes were lovely: toward connected self-reliance at the Irish Museum of Modern Art,* Irish Museum of Modern Art, Dublin.

FONDAZIONE FITZCARRALDO (2004), *Indagine sul Pubblico dei Musei Lombardi,* Regione Lombardi - Direzione Generale Culture, Identità e Autonomie, Milano.

FOURTEAU C. (ed.) (2000), *Les Institutions culturelles au plus près du public,* La Documentation Française - Musée du Louvre, Paris.

FREIRE P. (1977), *Cultural Action for Freedom*, Penguin, Middlesex.
– (1970), *Pedagogy of the Oppressed*, Penguin, London.

FRYER R. H. (1997), *Learning for the 21st century. First report of the National Advisory Group for continuous Education and lifelong learning*, National Advisory Group for continuous Education and lifelong learning
(also available on: www.lifelonglearning.co.uk/nagcell)

GABRIELLI C. (ed.) (2001), *Apprendere con il museo*, IRRSAE del Lazio - FrancoAngeli, Milano.

GLEASON M., SCHAUBLE L. (2000), *What do adults need to effectively assist children's learning?*, Museum Learning Collaborative, Studies of Learning from Museums.

GOULD H. (2005), *Where are they now? The impact of the Museums and Galleries Lifelong Learning initiative*, clmg/DfES.

GRAHAM J. (2001), *Family Interactions. Guidelines and Resources for catering for Families in museums*, West Midlands Regional Museums Council.

GROUP FOR LARGE LOCAL AUTHORITY MUSEUMS (2000), *Museums and Social Inclusion*, GLLAM Report, London.

HALL R. (2005), *Creative Evaluation Approaches*, The Hub
(available to download from http://www.collectandshare.eu.com/reports/index.aspx).

HANRAHAN S. (2003), *Equivalence*, Irish Museum of Modern Art, Dublin.

HARRIS QUALITATIVE (1997), *Children as an Audience for Museums and Galleries*, Museums and Galleries Commission and the Arts Council of England, Richmond Sy.

HEALTH DEVELOPMENT AGENCY (2000), Art for Health. A review of good practice in community-based arts projects and initiatives with impact on health and wellbeing, London.

HEIN G. (1998), *Learning in the Museum*, Routledge, London.

– (1982), «Evaluating museums education programmes», in *Art Galleries Association Bullettin*, September 1982, pp. 13-16.

HEIN H. (2000), *The Museum in Transition. A philosophical Perspective*, Smithsonian Institution Press, Washington and London.

HOGGART R. (2001), *Between Two Worlds*, Aurum Press, London.

HOOGSTRAAT E., VELS HEIJN A. (2006), *De leertheorie van Kolb in het museum. Dromer, Denker, Beslisser, Doener*, Museum Vereniging, Amsterdam.

HOOPER-GREENHILL E. (2000), *Museums and the interpretation of visual culture*, Routledge, London.
– (ed.) (1997), *Cultural diversity: developing museums audiences in Britain*, Leicester University Press, Leicester.
– (ed.) (1995), *Museum, Media, Message*, Routledge, London.
– (1994 a) *Museums and their visitors*, Routledge, London.
– (ed.) (1994 b), *The Educational Role of the Museum*, Routledge, London (2nd edition 1999).
– (1992), *Museum and the shaping of knowledge*, Routledge, London.
– (1991), *Museum and Gallery Education*, Leicester University Press, Leicester.

HOOPER-GREENHILL E., MOUSSOURI T. (2002), *Researching Learning in Museums and Galleries: a Bibliographic Review*, RCMG, Leicester.

HUTCHINSON J., Mc GONAGLE D. (1991), *Inheritance and Transformation*, Irish Museum of Modern Art, Dublin.

ICOM (2002), *Code of Ethics*, Paris.

ICOM CECA (1998), *Evaluation and museum education*, Paris.

ILCZUK D., ISAR R. (ed.) (2006), *Metropolises of Europe: diversity in urban cultural life*, CIRCLE Publication 14, Pro Cultura Foundation, Warsaw.

ILLERIS H. (2005), *Museums and Galleries as Performative Sites for Learning*, paper prepared for the Collect & Share international conference "Lifelong Learning in Museums and Galleries: a life-changing experience" (Stockholm, Moderna Museet, June 14th–18th, 2005)
(available to download from www.collectandshare.eu.com/reports/index.aspx)
– (2002), *The three dimensions of learning: contemporary learning theory in the tension field between the cognitive, the emotional and the social*, Roskilde University Press, Frederiksberg.

KOLB D. A. (2005), *Learning Style Inventory Version 3-1*, Hay Group, Boston.
– (1999), *Learning Style Inventory Version 3*, Hay Group, Boston.
– (1984), *Experiential learning. Experience as the Source of learning and Development*, Prentice Hall, New Jersey.

LANG C., REEVE J., WOOLARD V. (2006), *The Responsive Museum: working with audiences in the 21st century*, Ashgate Publishing Ltd., London.

MARSHALL C., O'DONOGHUE H. (2001), *Celebrating a Decade*, Irish Museum of Modern Art, Dublin.

MARTIN B. (ed.) (1999), *Adult education and the museum*, Final Report on the Socrates Project TM-AE 1-995-DE-1 supported by the DG XXII of the European Commission, DVV, Bonn.

MASCHERONI S. (2004), *Musei, disagi sociali e intercultura: storie di incontri, in Il museo come luogo dell'incontro. La didattica museale delle identità e delle differenze*, proceedings of the conference "VII Giornata Regionale di studio sulla didattica museale" (Vicenza, Palazzo Opere Sociali, November 24th , 2003), Regione Veneto.

MATARASSO, F. (1997), *Use or Ornament? The Social Impact of Participation in the Arts*, Comedia, London.

MATTOZZI I. (2000), «La didattica dei beni culturali: alla ricerca di una definizione», in M. Cisotto Nalon (ed.), *Il Museo come laboratorio per la scuola. Per una didattica dell'arte*, Il Poligrafo, Padova.

MINISTERO PER I BENI E LE ATTIVITÀ CULTURALI (2001), «Atto di indirizzo sui criteri tecnico-scientifici e sugli standard e sviluppo dei musei», in *Supplemento ordinario alla Gazzetta Ufficiale*, n. 244, 19 October 2001.

MOFFAT H., WOLLARD V. (1999), *Museum and gallery education: a manual of good practice*, The Stationery Office, London.

MOORE J. (1997), *Poverty, Access & Participation in the arts: a Regeneration*, A report by a working group funded by the Combat Poverty Agency and The Arts Council of Ireland, Dublin.

MORI (Market & Opinion Research International) (2004), *Visitors to Museums and Galleries*, Research Study Conducted for the Museums Libraries and Archives Council, MLA, London.

MUSEUMS ASSOCIATION (2002), *Code of Ethics for Museums: Ethical Principles for all who work or govern Museums in the UK*, London.
– (1999), *Ethical Guidelines: Access*, London.

MUSEUMS & GALLERIES COMMISSION, *Guidelines on Quality of service in Museums*, London.

NARDI E. (ed.) (2001), *Leggere il museo. Proposte didattiche*, SEAM, Roma.
– (1999), *Un laboratorio per la didattica museale*, SEAM, Roma.

NAYLOR C. (ed.) (2003), *The "Getting it Together" programme: "a very different energy?"*, engage, London.

O'DONOGHUE H. (2003), «Come to the Edge: Artists, Art and Learning at the Irish Museum of Modern Art – A Philosophy of Access and Engagement», in M. Xanthoudaki, L. Tickle, V. Sekules (ed.), *Researching Visual Arts Education in Museums and Galleries*, Kluwer Academic Publishers, London.
– (1999), *...and start to wear purple*, Irish Museum of Modern Art, Dublin.

POLICY ACTION TEAM reports 10 and 12, *Social Inclusion: A Response to Policy Action Team 10* (available to download from www.sportdevelopment. org.uk/html/pat10.htm and www.socialexclusionunit. gov.uk/page.asp?id=46).

POLLAK A. (1999), «Preface», in A. Davoren, H. O'Donoghue, *A Space to Grow: New approaches to working with children, primary school teachers and contemporary art in the context of a museum*, Irish Museum of Modern Art, Dublin.

PRINGLE E. (2006), *Learning in the Gallery: context, process, outcomes*, engage (available to download from www.en-quire.org and www.artscouncil.org.uk).

PROVINCIA DI MODENA - ASSESSORATO ALLA CULTURA (2004), *Il museo prossimo venturo*, conference proceedings (Modena, November 14th, 2003).

RANEY K. (ed.) (2006), *engage Journal 18, Research*, engage, London.
– (ed.) (2002), *engage Journal 11, Inclusion under Pressure*, engage, London.

RESOURCE (2003), *Measuring the Outcomes and Impact of Learning in Museums Archives and Libraries*. The Learning Impact Research Project, Leicester.
– (2001 a), *Mapping of Standards for Museums, Galleries, and Archives in the UK*, London.
– (2001 b), *Disability Directory for Museums and Galleries*, London.
– (2001 c), *Museum Learning Online: Guidelines for Good Practice*, London.
– (2000), *Responding to Cultural Diversity: Guidance for Museums and Galleries 2000*, London.
– (1995), *Registration Scheme for Museums and Galleries in the UK*, London.

RIBALDI, C. (ed.) (2005), *Il nuovo museo. Origini e percorsi*, vol. 1, il Saggiatore, Milano.

ROBERTS L. (1997), *From Knowledge to Narrative. Education and the Changing Museum*, Smithsonian Institution, Washington and London.

RUBENSON K. (2004), «Lifelong Learning: A Critical Assessment of the Political Project», in *Shaping an Emerging Reality – Researching Lifelong Learning*, Publication from the Graduate School in Lifelong Learning, Roskilde University Press, Frederiksberg.

SANDELL R. (2006), *Museums, Prejudice and the Reframing of Difference*, Routledge, London.
– (ed.) (2002), *Museums, Society, Inequality*, Routledge, London.
– (2000), «Means to and end: museums, galleries and social inclusion», in *Artsbusiness* 44, 14 February 2000.
– (1998), «Museums as Agents of Social Inclusion», in *Museum Management and Curatorship*, vol. 17, no. 4, pp. 401-418.

SANI M., TROMBINI A. (ed.) (2003), *La qualità nella pratica educativa al museo*, Compositori, Bologna.

SANI M. (ed.) (2004), *Musei e lifelong learning. Esperienze educative rivolte agli adulti nei musei europei*, Istituto Beni Culturali della Regione Emilia Romagna, Bologna.

SCOTT C. (2002), «Measuring Social Value», in R. Sandell (ed.), *Museums, Society, Inequality*, Routledge, London.

SERRELL B. (1996), *Exhibit Labels: an interpretative approach*, Altamira Press, Walnut Creek.

STANNET A., ST GER G. (ed.) (2001), *Museums, Keyworkers and Lifelong Learning: shared practice in five countries*, Buro fur Kulturvermittlung, Vienna.

SWIFT F. (1999), «Resources for informal and self-directed family learning», in *Museum Practice* 12, vol. 4, no. 3, pp. 40-42.

TORRINGA J. (2000), *Tekst bij beeld*, Museum Vereniging, Amsterdam.

THINESSE-DEMEL J. (ed.) (2005), *engage extra: Museums and Galleries as Learning Places*, engage (available to buy from engage or to download from http://www.engage.org/readmore/epublications.aspx).
– (ed.) (2001), *Education as a Tool for Museums*, Final Report on the Socrates Project MUSAEAM, Budapest.

THOMPSON J. (2002), *Bread and Roses Arts Culture and Lifelong Learning*, NIACE, Leicester.

TRIMARCHI M., LONGO F. (2004), «I musei italiani nel decennio: innovazioni e questioni irrisolte», in C. Bodo, C. Spada (ed.), *Rapporto sull'economia della cultura in Italia, 1990-2000*, Il Mulino, Bologna.

UNESCO (2001), *Universal Declaration on Cultural Diversity*.

USHER R. (2000), «Adult Education and Lifelong Learning in Postmodernity», in K. Illeris (ed.), *Adult Education in the Perspective of the Learners*, Roskilde University Press, Frederiksberg.

WILK C., HUMPHREY N. (ed.) (2004), *Creating the British Galleries at the V&A. A Study in Museology*, V&A Publications, London.

WOOLF, F. (1999), *Partnerships for Learning. A guide to evaluating arts education projects*, Regional Arts Boards and the Arts Council of England, London.

ZERBINI L. (ed.), (2006), *La didattica museale*, Aracne, Roma

Web sites

www.aam.org
(American Association of Museums)

www.ali.gov.uk
(Adult Learning Inspectorate)

www.beniculturali.it/sed/
(Sed - Il giornale del Centro per i Servizi educativi, Ministero per i Beni e le Attività Culturali)

www.clmg.org.uk
(The Campaign of Learning through Museums and Galleries)

www.coe.int
(Council of Europe)

www.collectandshare.eu.com
(Collect & Share)

www.culturalpolicies.net
(Compendium of Cultural Policies and Trends)

www.dcms.gov.uk
(Department for Culture, Media and Sports, UK)

www.dfes.gov.uk
(Department for Education and Skills, UK)

www.eaea.org
(European Association for the Education of Adults)

ekb.mwr.biz
(E-Learning Knowledge Base-E-Learning in Museums and the Tertiary Education Sector)

www.engage.org
(Engage)

www.euclid.info
(Euclid)

www.futurelab.org.uk
(Futurelab – Innovation in Education)

www.icom.org
(International Council of Museums)

www.insea.org
(INSEA – International Society for Education through Arts)

www.inspiringlearningforall.gov.uk
(Inspiring Learning For All)

www.labforculture.org
(Lab for Culture)

www.comune.torino.it/museiscuola
(museiscuol@)

www.mla.gov.uk
(Museums, Libraries And Archives Council, UK)

www.europeanmuseumforum.org
(European Museum Forum)

www.museumlearning.org
(Museum Learning Cooperative)

www.niace.org.uk
(NIACE – National Institute of Adult Continuing Education)

www.resource.gov.uk/action/registration/stdsmap.asp
(Resource)

www.unesco.org
(UNESCO)

Biographical notes

David Anderson is Director of Learning and Interpretation at the Victoria and Albert Museum, London.

Margaret O' Brien is Head of Lifelong Learning at the British Museum, London.

Judi Caton is a researcher, writer and museum consultant who after many years of working in museums in the UK is now based in Italy. She specialises in helping museums and museum workers to communicate better with the public, often through training.

Cristina Da Milano is a researcher who is working for Eccom, European Centre for Cultural Organisation and Management. She specialises in museum communication and education with specific reference to the theme of culture as a means of social integration.

Martina De Luca carries out research projects on modern and contemporary visual arts, with special interest for public and social art. She has been consultant for various Italian museums. She is President of Eccom (European Centre for Cultural Organization and Management) and lectures in Economics of Cultural Heritage and Activities at the University of Tuscia.

Helen O'Donoghue has held the post of Senior Curator: Head of Education and Community Programmes at the Irish Museum of Modern Art (IMMA) since its founding in 1991. She has piloted, designed and developed the framework for public access to all aspects of the Museum's programmes. She qualified in Fine Art, Painting, at the National College of Art and Design, Dublin, Ireland.

Juliette Fritsch is Head of Gallery Interpretation, Evaluation and Resources at the Victoria and Albert Museum, London. She has worked in visitor studies and researching interpretive techniques for several years, previously at English Heritage and Historic Royal Palaces.

Kirsten Gibbs is a museum and gallery consultant. She offers project management, professional development, training, and specialist advice in the field of museum and gallery education, interpretation and working with audiences. As Deputy Director of engage, the UK-based National Association for Gallery Education, Kirsten project-managed the Grundtvig 4 network, Collect & Share, promoting lifelong learning in European museums.

Rinske Jurgens has worked as a curator, designer and educator in several Dutch museums. She is now exhibition manager at the Maritime Museum Rotterdam (2001- ..) and she was responsible for STEM TO STERN - ship's decoration from bow to stern.

Kaija Kaitavuori is Head of Development, in the Art Museum Development Department of the Finnish National Gallery, Helsinki. Previously Head of education at the Contemporary Art Museum Kiasma, and responsible for the educational programmes and audience development work in the museum since its opening in1987.

Hanneke Kempen has been working at the Maritime Museum Rotterdam for ten years. She started as Coordinator Visitors Service, since the last two years she switched to museum education.

Andrea Kieskamp started as freelance guest curator at the Maritime Museum Rotterdam. Since 1997 she works as an exhibition manager. Her specialism is cultural diversity. She is focussing on script writing and is researching how to use this within exhibitions.

Massimo Negri European Museum Forum Director, since 1983, member of the Jury of the European Museum of the Year Award . Professor of Museology at the IULM Univeristy of Milan and at the M.A. in Industrial Archaeology at the University of Padua. He is also Consultant to the Province of Milan for museum programmes.

Carla Padró is Assistant Professor of Art Education at the University of Barcelona. She has collaborated with a number of pieces of educational research, including projects at the Corcoran Gallery of Art and Sites Gallery in Washington DC and the National Museum of Catalan Art.

Margarida Ruas is the Director of the Water Museum in Lisbon, the President of APOREM (Portuguese Association of Enterprises with Museums), National Correspondent for the European Museum Forum, Member of TICCHI ,Consultant of Lisbon International Club, Advisor of Orensanz Foundation in NY, teacher of Communication and Patrimony at Lusofona University and author of several articles in different areas of knowledge, namely lifelong learning in museums, environment, culture and published a book about political marketing.

Margherita Sani works at the Istituto Beni Culturali of the Region Emilia Romagna where she is in charge of several innovative and special projects, EU funded projects, training programmes for museum personnel, both at regional and international level.

Dineke Stam is an historian, specialised in gender and diversity. In the Anne Frank House she was a curator of exhibitions, researcher and project manager education. From 2001 till 2004 she headed Intercultural Programmes at the Netherlands Museum Association. Since 2004 she is an independent consultant for Intercultural Museum and Heritage Projects.

Jane Thompson is Principal Research Officer at NIACE. She has worked in adult education for many years and has leadership responsibility at NIACE for learning in relation to Arts and Culture.

Ineke van Klink was a museum educator for more than 20 years. She spent the last twelve years working as an exhibition manager specialised in interpretation methods. Among many exhibitions, four big interactive children's exhibitions were made by her.

Annemarie Vels Heijn has worked in museum education for more than 25 years. She was director of presentation at the Rijksmuseum in Amsterdam (1989-1998) and director of the Netherlands Museum Association (1998-2003). She now is an independent museum adviser and publishes on museum subjects.

Amber Walls is currently Development Coordinator of envision, engage's pioneering programme supporting galleries to develop youth-friendly practice. She has worked in a variety of roles broadly encompassing gallery education and the arts in community development contexts, and has specific expertise in engaging creatively with at risk young people.

Sue Wilkinson is Director of Learning, Access, Renaissance and the Regions at MLA (Museums, Libraries and Archives Council), London